W9-BYA-420

THE PRACTICAL GUIDE

CAT
AND
KITTEN CARE

A British Shorthair Red Tabby kitten

An odd-eyed White British Shorthair

THE PRACTICAL GUIDE TO

CAT
AND
KITTEN CARE

A complete illustrated guide to choosing and caring for your cat or kitten

David Alderton

Tetra🐾Press

No. 16041

A SALAMANDER BOOK

CREDITS

Published by Tetra Press
201 Tabor Road
Morris Plains, NJ 07950

ISBN 3-923880-77-4

Library of Congress Number:
87-050041

This book may not be sold outside the
United States of America and Canada

All correspondence concerning the
content of this volume should be
addressed to Tetra Press

Editor: Anthony Hall
Designer: Bob Mathias
Photographs: Marc Henrie, Hans
Reinhard, Bruce Coleman Ltd (pp 23,
top), John Walsh/Science Photo Library
(pp 84), Dr C J Smale/Science Photo
Library (pp 93)
Illustrations: Clive Spong
Colour illustration: Contemporary
Lithoplates Ltd
Typesetting: Interactive Photosetting

Printed in Portugal

AUTHOR

David Alderton
Trained as a veterinary surgeon at
Magdalene College, Cambridge and
began writing about pets and their care
during 1976. David has written several
books on cat care and contributes
regularly to various specialist periodicals
on the subject. He is involved in a
consultative capacity with the US-based
Pet Information Bureau and the Pet
Industry Joint Advisory Council as well
as with the European-based International
Pet Trade Organization. He has kept cats
for many years and is actively involved in
rehoming programmes.

CONTENTS

A Shorthair Blue-Cream

PHOTOGRAPHER   US CONSULTANT

Marc Henrie
Marc began his career as a Stills Man at the famous Ealing Film Studios in London. He then moved to Hollywood where he worked for MGM, RKO, Paramount and Warner Brothers.

Later, after he had retruned to England, Marc specialized in photographing dogs and cats, rapidly establishing an international reputation.

He has won numerous photographic awards, most recently the Kodak Award for the Best Animal Photograph and the Neal Foundation Award for Outstanding Photography of Animal Behaviour.

Marc is married to ex-ballet dancer, Fiona Henrie. They live in West London with their daughter Fleur, two Cavalier King Charles Spaniels and a cat called Topaz.

Shirlee Kalstone
Is the author of eight books and numerous articles on the grooming and care of dogs and cats. She is a member of the Empire Cat Club and is actively involved in Burmese and Egyptian Mau breeding. Mrs Kalstone has written the regular monthly grooming column for Pure-Bred Dogs, the American Kennel Club gazette, for several years and is the organizer of Intergroom, an international educational conference for groomers.

INTRODUCTION: CHOOSING A CAT

The domestic cat appears to have evolved in Egypt, about four thousand years ago, and was probably a descendant of the African Wild Cat *(Felis libyca).*

These cats feed largely on small mammals in the wild, and their presence was probably encouraged around grain stores in villages and cities, because of their hunting skills.

Soon a cult developed, based on the form of the cat-like goddess, Basht, and live cats acquired a religious significance. Many were apparently slaughtered for sacrificial purposes, to appease Basht, and entombed in special temples. Such events took place in the spring, and it seems likely that Basht, with the head of a cat and the body of a woman, was linked with fertility rites.

Since then the role of the domestic cat in society has varied through the ages. During times of plague, cats have been welcomed as a means of controlling the spread of vermin carrying deadly disease. Yet they have also been viewed as symbols of evil, linked with the occult and pagan worship, and have been persecuted as a result.

Superstition surrounding cats has survived until modern times. Even today, in the English county of Cornwall for example, ancient custom states that a cross should be drawn on the toe of a shoe, if you encounter an unknown black cat.

Towards the end of the 19th century the keeping of companion animals underwent a noticeable change, and this affected the cat as well as other creatures in this category. The rise of the fancy meant that emphasis was then placed on selective breeding, and this saw the emergence of specific breeds which possessed common recognizable features.

Competitive exhibitions attracted support, and here cats were shown and judged to the prescribed standards for their breeds. In Britain, the first National Cat Show took place in 1871, and a similar event was organized 24 years later in the United States.

Since that time the cat has tended to be viewed more as a companion,

Above: European Wild Cat (Felis sylvestris), *a species which has been crossed with domestic cats.*

rather than a working animal serving to control vermin. At the present time, the cat population is growing dramatically throughout Europe and North America, mirroring social changes. As there are now more households, with fewer members on average, so the independent nature of the pet cat assumes greater appeal.

Cats are less demanding in terms of their care than dogs, and can prove well-suited to living in towns. Indeed, it is possible to keep cats permanently indoors, whereas this does not apply to dogs.

With a growing number of elderly people in society, the appeal of the cat as a companion is further strengthened since, unlike dogs, cats do not require regular periods of exercise.

Owning a cat
You should never obtain a cat unless you can be certain that you will have adequate time to care for it properly. It will need regular feeding, as well as grooming, particularly in the case of a longhaired cat. Costs of ownership will be increased by inevitable veterinary expenses, such as inoculations, and possibly by cattery fees when you are away from home.

Furthermore, although cats are rather more self-reliant than dogs, they will appreciate affection being bestowed on them, and you must make time for this every day, assuming that you really want a companion animal.

Otherwise, your intended pet is likely to end up swelling the feral cat populations which are now present in most major cities, and will be destined to have a short life. The life expectancy of such cats may not exceed two years, whereas household pets can live ten times longer, and, very occasionally, a few individuals may survive up to 30 years of age.

The physical cat

All the wild animals of the cat family are specialists in hunting, and the marks of this are clearly seen in their domestic counterpart. Cats are predatory by nature, and cannot survive without a meat diet (including fish); they are well equipped for hunting prey. Their body is lithe, a feature emphasized in certain breeds such as the popular Siamese, yet powerful, enabling a cat to run fast, especially over a short distance.

The agility of the cat also enables it

Below: *The size of the cat's pupils can alter, depending on its mood and the prevailing light conditions.*

to jump and climb quite easily. Even if it loses its balance, the cat is normally able to adjust its fall so that it invariably lands on its feet, minimizing the risk of spinal injury as a result, although the impact may damage its lower jaw.

Similarly, having climbed up a tree, the cat can simply reverse its position and leap down to the ground. Cats may well walk away uninjured after leaping from a height of 6m (20ft), although such behaviour is obviously not to be encouraged.

Being equipped physically to capture its victims, the cat must also be able to locate potential prey accurately, without revealing its presence until the last moment before it strikes. It is not surprising therefore that the eyesight of the cat is highly developed, serving not only to recognize prey, but also to pinpoint its position with a very high degree of accuracy, maximizing the likelihood of a lethal strike.

The pupils, which are the black areas at the centre of both eyes, are very sensitive to light intensity, opening to form broad circles when the lighting level is low. This permits the maximum amount of light to

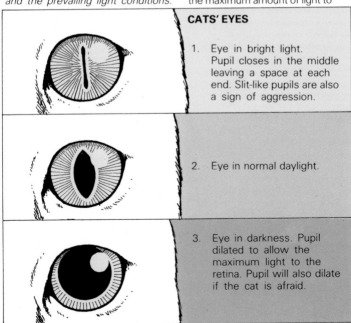

CATS' EYES

1. Eye in bright light. Pupil closes in the middle leaving a space at each end. Slit-like pupils are also a sign of aggression.

2. Eye in normal daylight.

3. Eye in darkness. Pupil dilated to allow the maximum light to the retina. Pupil will also dilate if the cat is afraid.

penetrate to the retina at the back of the eye, where the image is formed.

As hunters, cats are well suited to a nocturnal existence, because they possess an additional layer, known as the tapetum lucidum, behind the retina of each eye. As a result, light rays which have fallen on the cells present in the retina are immediately reflected back again to the retina, and this serves to reinforce the image here. The presence of the tapetum lucidum accounts for the typically greenish and glowing appearance of cats' eyes when they are caught in the beam of car headlamps after dark.

There are two groups of cells present on the cat's retina, known as rods and cones. The rods respond to much lower levels of light intensity, and thus assist with vision when there is little light penetrating the retina. The ratio of rods to cones is considerably higher in cats than humans, so they can see well when there is relatively poor light. A cat is therefore able to see in an environment where human eyes are only able to receive an image of total darkness.

Other hunting adaptations

As in humans and dogs, each of the cat's eyes receive a slightly different image, with a central area of overlap. This provides the basis for binocular vision, enabling the cat to identify the position of its prey with great certainty. However, in domestic cats this ability varies according to the breed concerned, and young kittens lack binocular vision. Their hunting skills are therefore compromised as a result , and they are not able to catch prey until they are about three months old.

Cats have a highly developed sense of smell, which can help to locate other cats, as well as prey. Scent molecules wafted on the air become trapped on the tongue, and this in turn makes contact with Jacobsen's organ, which is located in the roof of the mouth. A direct link connects to the brain, so that scents acquired in this way can be interpreted quickly, thus enabling appropriate action to be taken by the cat.

Having pounced on prey, the cat's retractable claws are used to hold on to the unfortunate creature, enabling the sharp, pointed canine teeth at the front of the cat's mouth to be used to deadly effect. The papillae, which are the tiny protrusions on the cat's tongue, creating its rough feel, can also help to grasp small prey.

Even the cat's taste buds (also situated on the tongue) reflect its lifestyle. Cats cannot taste sweet

Above: *The lethal canine teeth of the cat are clearly displayed by this Scottish Wild Cat.*

Left: *A cream Burmese stalking potential prey. Hunting instincts can remain strong in the most domesticated of pet cats.*

foods, which in the wild they would not encounter, but they will recognize drinking water via taste buds located on specific papillae. These tend to be sited around the outer rim of the tongue.

The tongue itself serves as a ladle when necessary, becoming expanded and curled at its tip as the cat drinks. In this way, more fluid can be consumed in a shorter space of time. The cat therefore needs to spend less time at the water, where it could be vulnerable to other potential predators while drinking.

Further sensory input is derived from the whiskers. These not only detect physical barriers, but also pick up the direction of the prevailing wind. This in turn can be of great value for hunting purposes.

Preliminary decisions for cat owners

Several decisions will need to be taken before you actually start to look for your cat, as these will almost certainly affect where you obtain your new pet. In the first place, you will have to decide whether or not you want a pedigree cat. There are numerous breeds to choose from, and these can differ significantly in terms of both appearance and temperament.

The following is a selection of the

THE ANATOMY OF CLAWS

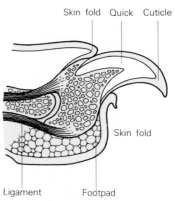

UNSHEATHING THE CLAWS

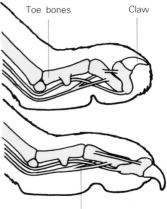

Tendons connecting toe bones with leg muscles

Above: *Claws grow continuously from below the upper skin fold of the paw, and as part of the skin. The claw is held within a sheath of skin in the paw by an elastic ligament. To unsheath the claws, muscles in the leg contract, pulling on tendons which pull the claw forward.*

This unique characteristic of cats is an essential aid to hunting as is their way of moving on their toes, known as digitigrade posture.

breeds most likely to be encountered. Do bear in mind, though, that individuals may differ somewhat in price, even within a particular breed.

If you are not looking for a show cat, you may be lucky enough to find a breeder who has one or two cats that may have a fault rendering them unsuitable for exhibition purposes, yet are perfectly healthy. Such individuals are often sold cheaply to a pet-seeker.

Clearly, if you obtain your pet from a renowned bloodline, you will pay more for the individual cat, but unless you want to show or breed from your pet at a later date, there is no real advantage to such a purchase.

Cat breeds and varieties

Abyssinian: This breed appears to have originated in the Nile Valley, and was first introduced to Europe at the end of the last century. It is characterized by its sleek appearance, a feature emphasized by its soft fur. The ears of the Abyssinian are another distinctive trait, being relatively broad yet pointed, contributing to the breed's lively appearance.

The unusual colour of the Abyssinian results from the contrasting dark and coloured areas present on each individual hair. This is described as ticking. In the traditional form, the fur is ruddy brown with black markings.

Mutations have since occurred, and a russet or red form, with a coppery-red body coloration, offset against several bands of ticking, has now been developed. Other less common colour variants include Silver and Blue Abyssinians. A long-haired form of the Abyssinian, described as the Somali, is becoming increasingly popular at present: apart from having a longer coat, its hair is also somewhat silkier than that of the Abyssinian itself.

These cats are justifiably popular as pets, possessing rather a foreign appearance, and yet being temperamentally quite placid and quiet. The breed has suffered badly in the past from feline leukaemia, so check carefully on this aspect before purchase. Most breeding stock will be screened regularly for the presence of the virus.

Above: *A red Burmese. This is one of the newer colour varieties; they are also sometimes decribed as Malayans.*

American Wirehair: The distinctive feature of this North American breed is its rough, crimped coat, which will fold back into position after being touched. The mutation first appeared in the United States during 1966, and was established there. Similar cats were known in Britain previously, having appeared in a colony of feral cats inhabiting a derelict bomb site, but the characteristic was not fixed in this case. Wirehairs are hardy, affectionate cats, but the appearance and feel of their coat does not appeal to all.

Angora (Turkish Angora): This is an old breed, of Turkish origin, which has been known in Europe for centuries. These are cats of elegant proportions, and they have active, playful natures. Yet while breed weaknesses are not as common in pedigree cats as in pedigree dogs, you must be careful in this instance. Like all pure white cats, the Angora, if blue-eyed, is likely to be deaf, because of a congenital defect affecting the organ of Corti, in the middle ear. In the United States the Cat Fanciers' Association (CFA) recognized only white Angoras until

Above: *Blue Abyssinians. The blue is a less common variety of this popular breed, which is many centuries old.*

1978, but now a variety of colours is acceptable.

It is believed that the Odd-eyed White, known in its Turkish homeland as *Ankara kedi,* is the original form of this breed. Such cats usually have partial hearing, being deaf only in the ear on the side of the head corresponding with their blue eye.

Birman: These cats also are of ancient lineage, being considered sacred in their Burmese homeland. The first members of the breed seen in Europe were given to two travellers who helped to defend a temple from attack at the start of the present century.

Birmans have since been bred in a range of colours, and must show the foot and leg markings characteristic of the breed. The white areas on the front feet are described as gloves. In contrast those on the hind limb are more extensive, starting as so-called gauntlets which terminate in narrow laces at the back of the legs.

The longish, silky coat of this breed will require regular grooming to maintain its attractive appearance. One point to remember when obtaining a Birman kitten is that they mature earlier than other cats, and queens may be fertile when only seven months old.

Bombay: In spite of its exotic name, this is a composite breed which was developed in the United States, beginning in the late 1950s. It originated from American Shorthairs crossed with Burmese, and is still relatively uncommon. The Bombay possesses a distinctive short black coat, which should resemble patent leather in appearance, offset against coppery eyes.

Although attractive, these cats can be temperamental, and may therefore not be suited to a home where there are young children.

Burmese: This breed was again bred initially in the United States, using a queen which had originated in Burma. It was thought that such cats were simply dark Siamese, and undoubtedly this popular breed played a role in its development.

Today, however, the Burmese has a distinctive appearance, with a more rotund body shape than that of its likely relative. It has become extremely popular, and has been bred in many colours, although traditional Burmese enthusiasts still favour the Brown variety. Indeed, the new-coloured Burmese are sometimes described separately as Malayans.

15

The Burmese bears no relationship to the Birman, and its care is made more straightforward by the fact that it is short-coated. These cats make ideal companions, being both affectionate and playful by nature. During the course of a game, they may even retrieve the toy for their owner, and have been christened 'dog cats'.

Egyptian Mau: The actual markings of this breed are vital for exhibition purposes, so you may be able to obtain a mis-marked individual as a pet without too much difficulty. The markings actually vary in colour, depending upon the colour of the cat. The most distinctive feature of this breed is the presence of a dark 'M'-shaped marking in the centre of the forehead, with other darker areas distributed over much of the rest of the body.

Egyptian Maus resemble the Abyssinian in type, and originated in the same part of the world, as their name suggests. Their short, sleek coat serves to emphasize their lively dispositions. While affectionate with members of their immediate circle, these cats will not readily accept strangers as a general rule.

Foreign Colours: This group of cats, described in the United States as Oriental Shorthairs, is derived from Siamese stock, but the cats differ significantly in their coloration. Traditionally, two varieties are acceptable in this category in Britain, whereas in North America, a much wider range of colours can be included under this heading.

The cats themselves resemble Siamese closely, both in terms of their physical appearance (also described as 'type') and temperament. Indeed, watch for the faults traditionally associated with Siamese, notably squinting, and any trace of a kinked tail, when acquiring one of these cats.

Havana: Here, as in other cases, the breed has developed in different ways on opposite sides of the Atlantic. British Havanas are more directly related to the variety known as the Oriental Self Brown, resembling their original Siamese ancestors. In North America, however, a different type of cat has evolved, with a relatively cobby

Above: *Foreign White, or Oriental Shorthair. These cats resemble the Siamese in looks and temperament*

(stocky) body outline and a more placid temperament.

Himalayan Longhair: Better known in Britain as the Colourpoint Longhair, such cats arose from Siamese/Longhair crosses, and have been bred to retain the qualities of both

ancestors. They are available in all the usual Siamese colours, and their coats will require the grooming associated with other longhaired breeds.

It is particularly hard to assess a kitten's likely adult coloration in this breed, as with the Siamese, because the colour of the body extremities, known as points, will not be fully apparent until the cat in question is perhaps 18 months old.

Do not be surprised either if Himalayan kittens have relatively short coats: this is quite usual, and the coat will continue growing up to a maximum length of 12cm (5in). Indeed, the overall type of these cats is more akin to that of the Longhair, while its markings resemble those of the Siamese.

Himalayans tend to be sexually precocious, compared with other longhaired cats, but are reasonably docile in terms of temperament.

Longhairs (Persians): A large selection of Longhairs, or Persians, can be seen at cat shows. They have been bred in a very wide range of colours, ranging from black to cream, and blue to red. Apart from these self (solid) colours, various colour combinations are also recognized, including Tortoiseshell and White, and various Tabby forms.

Colour is essentially a matter of personal preference, but if you are thinking of obtaining one of these cats, do be prepared to devote a period each day to grooming your pet. Without such care, not only will their overall appearance suffer and their hair become badly matted, but they are more likely to suffer from hair-balls, which can cause digestive problems.

Another point to bear in mind, especially if any members of your family suffer from asthma, is that allergies to cats are not that uncommon. People who have the misfortune to suffer from this affliction tend to be more susceptible to the

Below: *Blue Longhair with kitten. Be prepared for lengthy grooming sessions with longhairs to stop their coats becoming matted.*

symptoms of runny eyes and difficulty in breathing when in the company of longhaired cats.

If you have any doubts in this respect, therefore, it may be better to consider a shorthaired cat, preferably one of the Rex breeds which do not moult in the conventional sense. You should also ask your doctor for advice.

In terms of their temperament, Longhairs will make good companions, especially for elderly owners, because they tend to be very placid, and are home-loving by nature. They are also fairly tolerant, and thus can be recommended for a home where young children are present.

Nevertheless, both parties will need to be supervised as all cats are capable of expressing disapproval of the way they are being handled.

Maine Coon: A hardy North American breed, developed initially in the state of Maine. They were popular farm cats, being active hunters, but are now widely kept just as pets. The Maine Coon is a large breed, of which the tabby form is probably most commonly seen. In spite of their rough-looking coat, the texture of the fur of these cats is quite silky.

Manx: One of the best-known breeds of pedigree cat, the Manx is closely associated with the Isle of Man, off the west coast of England, where it is believed to have originated several centuries ago. Its precise origins are unknown. Although it is usually assumed that these cats are tailless, this is not a standard characteristic of the breed.

Some Manx cats have a tail almost as long as that of a normal cat and are called 'Longies' as a result. 'Stumpies' still have a clear vestige of the tail, but the ideal is considered to be a 'Rumpie', a Manx with no trace of the coccygeal vertebrae protruding as a tail.

This typical shortening of the vertebral column actually gives rise to the curved shape of the Manx's back. These cats have an unusual hopping gait, again because of their spinal malformation. A longhaired version of the Manx has been developed separately in the United States, where it is known as the Cymric.

The Manx is a hardy, unusual breed. They usually prove both intelligent and long-lived, and can be kept quite satisfactorily in the home. These cats also appear to agree well with dogs, especially if both are obtained at the same time when young. The colour of the Manx varies widely, so you should be able to find an individual which appeals to you.

They can be at risk from persistent constipation however, because of a reduction in the diameter of their anus, so check for this defect when examining stock of this breed.

Rexes: The two forms of Rex cat were bred in the English counties of Devon and Cornwall, and have been named accordingly. The Cornish Rex is the older type, being bred for the first time a decade before the appearance of its Devonian counterpart in 1960. Both have thin, curly coats, which give rise to their attractive name of poodle cats. Even their whiskers are affected.

The coat of the Devon Rex tends to be the thinnest of the two, but these breeds can be easily distinguished by their ears. Devon Rexes have broader ears and less prominent noses when compared with the Cornish breed.

Rexes are ideal as pets, especially for apartment owners, since they do not moult in the same way as other cats. Furthermore, their thin coats mean that they are not hardy, and Rexes are best protected against the elements. Keep a watch on the ears of these cats, since they are likely to become dirty, and will have to be cleaned regularly as a result.

Left: *Maine Coon. Still best-known in North America, this breed is also seen in Europe.*

Right: *Devon Rex, characterized by its broad ears and sparse curly coat. This breed is not very hardy.*

Below: *Cornish Rex. A longer nose and narrower ears differentiate it from the Devon Rex.*

Right: *British Shorthair. This is an example of the red tabby, popular both as a pet and as a show cat.*

Russian Blue: This breed was first brought to Europe around the middle of the last century by seamen returning from Russia. Since then the original type of the breed has been altered noticeably, as breeders fought to ensure its survival after the Second World War, when stock became short.

The introduction of Siamese blood led to Russian Blues with a more foreign appearance than had previously been acceptable, but now this trend has been reversed. The breed is generally affectionate and quiet by nature.

The grooming of these cats for exhibition purposes differs somewhat from the normal, in order to maintain their erect coat. Never flatten the coat by brushing in the direction of the fur, but start by grooming against the natural lie of the hair. Then comb it back lightly in its usual manner.

As might be expected, with its dense coat, the Russian Blue is a hardy breed, showing no sign of discomfort outside in cold weather.

A separate White form, which enjoys a strong following in Australia, is less common elsewhere at present.

Shorthairs: These cats are basically of working ancestry, with American, British and European forms being recognized. They are stocky in build. Although Shorthairs may not have the exotic appearance of certain breeds, they are very attractive, and as they are available in a wide range of colours,

Above: *Blue-point Siamese. The term 'point' refers to the darker extremities on the body.*

Below: *Siamese; the seal form of the Tortie-point. There are many such new varieties.*

you are certain to find a variety which appeals to you.

They range from colours such as blue and cream to tabbies and tortoiseshells. As might be expected from their background, Shorthairs are easy to care for, and make robust, affectionate companions.

Siamese: One of the best-known of the cat breeds, the Siamese is of oriental origin, although the precise details of its ancestry are unclear. They were brought to Britain at the end of the last century, and proved delicate at first. Furthermore, breeders did not take readily to them, but today they enjoy a widespread following.

Siamese have an unmistakably angular head, with quite large ears. Their body shape is lithe yet muscular, contributing to their elegant appearance. The so-called points of this breed are another important feature. These extremities, comprising the ears and mask on the head, plus the paws, lower legs and tail, are significantly darker, creating an attractive contrast with the lighter overall body coloration.

The traditional form of the Siamese is the Seal-point, with its bright blue eyes, and dark seal-brown points, offset against a paler brownish body. Other traditional colours include the Chocolate-point, which is a darker shade of brown than the Seal-point, and the Blue-point, with bluish-grey points. Lilac-points have glacial-white body coats with frosty pink-tinged grey points. They are a combination of chocolate and blue, and are one of the harder colours to breed satisfactorily for show purposes.

In addition, a number of new-coloured Siamese have been evolved during recent years, and these are often described as Colourpoint Shorthairs, notably in North America. The development of such cats has entailed crossing with other breeds to modify the coloration of the points.

Then, once the desired characteristics have been introduced, Siamese are used exclusively to modify the type of the emerging variety to correspond as closely as possible to that of other Siamese. Amongst the new colours in this group

Above: *A chocolate tabby Siamese, a breed recognised in North America as a form of the Colorpoint Shorthair.*

are Tortie-point Siamese and Tabby (Lynx)-pointed Siamese.

The appeal of the Siamese is not confined to its appearance however, and they can prove very demonstrative cats. Individuals do vary in terms of temperament, but they tend to be very lively, intelligent and also sexually precocious. Siamese are especially vocal cats, and although highly affectionate, may prove aggressive if aroused.

They are therefore most suited to a home without young children, and they also may not agree well with dogs, although there are of course exceptions. Careful introductions are to be recommended in any event, so as to prevent the likelihood of disagreements.

When purchasing a Siamese cat, check that it is unaffected by squinting. Such cats tend to appear as if they are staring constantly at their noses, which is usually quite evident. Another traditional flaw associated with this breed is kinking of the tail. Since these faults are of genetic origin, such animals should be excluded from breeding programmes.

Do not be surprised, though, when the points of Siamese kittens appear much paler than those of adult cats. This is quite usual, and the depth of coloration increases as the kitten matures. Indeed, for this reason, Siamese tend to have relatively short show careers, because their body coloration overall becomes too dark

Above: *Brown and white tabby. The distinctive tabby markings have been introduced to various breeds.*

Below: *The Turkish Van is an unusual breed of great character which appears to like water.*

to conform to the required standard while they are still quite young.

Bear in mind that Siamese are active and agile cats. They will climb around a room more than other breeds. If you live in an urban area and do not wish to let your pet outside to exercise

Above: *The Sphynx, is known as the hairless cat, since it has virtually no hair. This variety is light blue.*

without close supervision, it is possible to train Siamese to walk on a leash. Obtain a harness and leash and encourage your cat to wear the harness at first around the home.

You can then exercise it on the leash, but keep the cat away from dogs which may be attracted to it, otherwise the fiery temper of Siamese is likely to be revealed.

Sphynx: While Rex cats retain a thin coat, the Sphynx is in fact virtually hairless. This mutation originated in Canada, and such cats are still quite scarce. They are not favoured for show purposes but can be very valuable for owners who are allergic to the hair of other breeds.

The Sphynx has striking golden eyes and, although its appearance is in no way attractive, these cats can become great companions. They are best kept indoors, certainly in cold climates, since they have no

protection against the elements.

In addition, without a layer of fur, they are potentially more at risk from injury if they come into conflict with other cats.

Turkish Van: While most cats will not bathe readily, the Turkish Van is a notable exception to this rule. It is thought to be related to the Angora, being discovered in Turkey as recently as 1955. The appearance of the Turkish Van alters quite noticeably through the year, since in summer it loses its thick winter coat and comes to resemble a shorthaired cat.

The combination of auburn markings on the head and tail, offset against white body coloration, creates an attractive contrast. At present, however, Turkish Vans are not widely available, and it may be difficult to obtain stock of this unusual breed.

Cross-breds: The physical differences between the various breeds of cats are far less noticeable than in the case of dogs. Indeed, the majority of cat owners do not choose a pedigree cat. They prefer a cross-bred, of no fixed ancestry.

Such cats are freely available, and prove equally acceptable as companions compared with their more illustrious counterparts. Indeed, they may be more suitable in certain instances, since cross-bred cats, affectionately described as 'moggies', are usually fairly tolerant by nature.

Where to look for a cat

It will be much easier to obtain a cross-bred cat than a pedigree animal. You can visit one of the animal welfare organizations, which frequently have such cats requiring good homes. They may insist on checking your suitability as a potential owner and may even visit you at home beforehand.

This should not be a cause for offence, and is certainly no reflection on you personally. Such visits are standard policy for many of these organizations. Their aim is simply to ensure that the cat will receive a permanent, loving home.

Most people prefer to obtain a young kitten rather than an adult cat. A kitten will usually tend to integrate better into unfamiliar domestic surroundings, compared with an older individual, which is more likely to stray when first let outside. It may well take longer to win the confidence of such cats, and it will be almost certainly impossible to estimate the age of a stray unless its history is known.

With a young cat, the teeth may help to judge its age. Baby teeth begin falling out between 3-4 months, as the permanent set starts pushing out through the gums. The incisors appear first, followed by the canines at five months and the premolars at six months. By seven months the permanent teeth should be in place. After this stage there is no reliable method of judging age.

If you do obtain your kitten from an animal welfare organization, make a

Above: A Somali queen with her litter. Pedigree kittens may be expensive to buy.

donation to their funds, since they are voluntary bodies without access to large budgets.

You may alternatively be attracted to a kitten in a pet store, which of course you will have to purchase. The major drawback of obtaining a kitten from either an animal welfare organization or a pet store is identical. There are likely to be a number of other cats on the same premises, which may represent a health threat, to a young kitten in particular.

Diseases can spread quite rapidly under such conditions, where animals from various backgrounds are brought together, and are often stressed as a result. A thorough health check assumes greater importance under these circumstances.

The risk of disease is dramatically reduced if you go direct to a breeder who has a litter of kittens available. You can see the surroundings in which the cats have been reared, and will be able to ascertain their background more easily. Advertisements offering litters of kittens often appear in local papers, or a veterinarian may be able to assist you in contacting a breeder.

For a pedigree kitten, you may need to get in touch with one of the registration authorities, such as the Governing Council of the Cat Fancy in Britain (GCCF), or the Cat Fanciers' Association (CFA) in the USA.

Above: *Cat shows provide an ideal way of seeing the various breeds and making contact with breeders.*

Below: *Judging in progress at a cat show. The various breeds must conform to certain standards.*

They should be able to direct you to someone who keeps the breed which appeals to you, possibly in your neighbourhood. In the case of more unusual breeds, however, you will almost certainly have to travel some distance to visit a breeder. The availability of such kittens is likely to vary, and you may have to be content with a place on a waiting list in the first instance.

One of the best ways to see different breeds, and contact breeders, is to visit a cat show. These events are held in many localities, and at larger shows you can expect a good range of breeds. Various cat periodicals are produced regularly,

although some can only be obtained on subscription. These give details of such shows, and also feature advertisements from breeders.

Certainly if you are interested in showing your kitten at a later stage, you should visit shows before making any decisions, so you can talk to breeders, and gain insight into what judges are looking for in the breed concerned. Written standards give far less guidance in this crucial area than looking at the cats themselves.

It may be possible in certain cases to acquire a kitten on breeding terms, entering into an agreement with the breeder concerned. Many cat exhibitors operate on a relatively small scale, and do not have the space or the finance to keep all the kittens which they breed.

The offspring from a particular litter may therefore be 'homed' on the basis that once they are mature, the kittens might be used for breeding purposes themselves. They remain the property of the breeder, or at least are part-owned, and mutual agreement is reached over such details as the choice of a stud tom.

An agreement of this type has obvious advantages to both parties, but a written contract is to be recommended, at the outset. This will help to prevent any disputes arising at a later date.

The gender

Generally, female cats or queens are the subject of a breeding agreement of this type, but in any event, you will need to consider the gender of the cat carefully, as this will obviously be significant later.

Domestic cats do differ from many mammals since males (known as toms) do not possess an external penis, but examination of the genital area will provide the necessary information to determine the cat's gender.

Female kittens have the slit-like opening of the vulva located almost directly below the anus. In contrast, males show a slightly raised area here, which forms the scrotum in the adult cat. Beneath this is the circular opening in which the penis is concealed. Even in a male cat which has been neutered this distinction can still be drawn, although obviously the scrotal sacs will not be apparent.

It can be much harder to distinguish whether or not a female cat has been spayed. Your veterinarian may be able to detect scar tissue on the flank or in the midline, depending on how the operation was carried out.

If you hope to exhibit your kitten at a later date, it will clearly be preferable to obtain a young queen, which can be mated once she is older. It is generally accepted that female cats do tend to be more affectionate than toms, and will be less prone to straying and fighting. Nevertheless, these problems in toms can be overcome to a great extent by neutering.

A major drawback of keeping an intact tom is that it will attempt to mark its territory by spraying urine, even inside the house, but this will also be cured by neutering. Such behaviour is not confined just to male cats

Below: *Like kittens of all breeds these lilac Burmese are lively and playful by nature.*

SEXING KITTENS

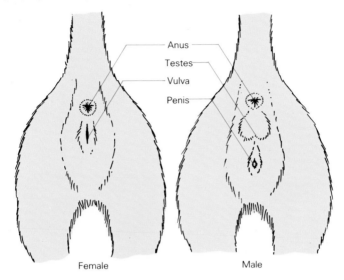

Anus
Testes
Vulva
Penis

Female   Male

however, and can be a problem even with queens.

In addition, unless they are neutered, females are almost certain to end up pregnant in a relatively short space of time, because of the nature of the unusual reproductive cycle of cats (see page 66).

Some breeds, such as the Siamese, are also liable to prove extremely vocal in the home during the breeding period.

Surgical neutering is a relatively safe operation in either sex, but it will inevitably be more straightforward, and cheaper, in the case of tom cats.

Choosing the right cat

When you are actually trying to select a kitten or cat, do not rush your choice. Look at the litter of kittens for a few moments. Note how they are behaving. Some may appear more dominant than others at this stage. One or two could be smaller in size, compared with their littermates. Clearly, these are not to be recommended, particularly for those seeking a show cat.

Other impressions may not be entirely reliable: one kitten may appear more lively or inquisitive than

Above: In male kittens, the scrotal area is clearly evident above the internal penis and below the anus.

another, yet it could be that it has just woken up and is at present more active. Cats tend to sleep for relatively long periods in any event, so that a kitten which is fast asleep will not necessarily be ill in any way.

For a more balanced view of the litter, you may do better to rely on the advice of the vendor. They will have seen the kittens grow up, and will have a better idea of their individual personalities as a result. Almost certainly, there will be a favourite member of the litter, which they themselves would pick as a pet.

Always ask before handling any of the kittens, although no prospective vendor should object to this request. Lift the kitten gently, providing adequate support beneath its body, and transfer it to a firm surface, so you can examine it more easily. Clearly, by this stage even a sleeping kitten should have woken up, unless it is actually unwell. Start at the head, and check that the nose shows no sign of discharge.

You may want to look inside the

mouth as well. This can be achieved by holding the top jaw at either side over the nasal bridge, using the thumb and first finger of one hand. Then gently prize down the lower jaw, keeping the head in a fairly vertical position.

The relative position of the jaws is an important point to check, especially in Siamese, which can be afflicted with malocclusion (when the upper jaw overlaps the lower).

Check also the paws, as in some cases there may be an extra toe. Described as being polydactyl, such cats are not handicapped in any way, but will be unsuitable for show purposes, where this dominant trait is penalized. Since it is genetically transmitted, they should not be used for breeding either.

When examining Siamese kittens and similar breeds, you may also note that kittens kept indoors may have paler points than those housed in outside catteries. This is simply because the gene responsible for this feature is temperature sensitive, and the coloration tends to become darker in a cool environment.
Alterations to point colour can result from bandaging, which serves to raise the local temperature around the foot, leading to paler fur coloration here.

The eyes of the kitten are especially important in white cats as explained previously, since those with blue eyes are likely to be deaf. Before this fact was appreciated, such kitten's were assumed to be less intelligent than those of other colours. Deafness is liable to prove a handicap for cats living in urban areas. They are likely to be less aware of traffic, for example, which can have fatal results.

Although this weakness will not be apparent from looking into the ears, check here nevertheless for any accumulations of dirt which will need to be removed. The eyes themselves must be clear, and free of any discharge. In particular, the third 'eyelid' or nictitating membrane should not extend across the eye.

The fur can conceal various parasites, such as fleas, and gently brushing this back with your hand against the natural lie of the coat will often reveal their presence. Look for

Above: *Choosing a kitten can be difficult. Obviously, though, it must appear healthy. Watch the litter for a while before taking any decisions and check the chosen kitten for parasites and congenital problems.*

Right: *It will be several weeks before these Siamese kittens can go to new homes, but already, at two weeks old, differences in their temperaments are evident.*

specks of blackish dirt, typically little bigger than a pin-head. Treatment of fleas is relatively straightforward, but you will also need to deworm the cat at the same time, since fleas transmit tapeworms.

You may gain an indication of the presence of internal parasites by looking at the kitten's belly. If this is fairly prominent, it often suggests a

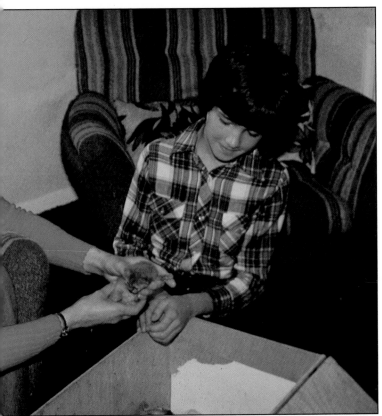

heavy burden of roundworms.

As you run your hand over this part of the body, check that it is not excessively thin, with the ribs being very prominent. Weight loss tends to be more evident in shorthaired cats.

Litters can sometimes be affected by an umbilical hernia, which will be apparent as a swelling in the mid-line on the underside of the body. On occasions, surgery may be required to overcome this problem, if the protrusion of tissue becomes noticeable for any reason. Such kittens can prove a source of subsequent concern therefore, and treatment may not be covered by a veterinary insurance scheme.

29

The final point to check is the anal region, holding the tail vertically for this purpose. The surrounding fur should not be matted, as this tends to indicate a digestive upset. Check the litter tray if you suspect there could be a problem, and bring this point to the vendor's attention. Kittens' faeces are usually firm, but sometimes, after deworming for example, temporary diarrhoea may result.

If you observe any whitish, rice-like pieces around the anus, these are liable to be tapeworm segments. Deworming of the individual concerned will be required. Indeed, always ask the vendor when the kitten or cat was last treated for intestinal parasites, since this information will probably be helpful in due course to your veterinarian.

You will also need to know what inoculations, if any, have been given, and when further boosters are due. This information may be present on a vaccination certificate which you will need to keep safely.

Further paperwork is likely to be necessary when you obtain a pedigree kitten or cat. The ancestry of the cat will feature on the pedigree certificate, which you should be given, and you will also have to complete a transfer form. This will need to be sent to the appropriate registration body, and serves to notify the authorities of the change of ownership.

In all cases, you should also obtain a diet sheet, setting out the food and feeding routine which the cat has been used to, so that you can follow a similar pattern. It can of course be altered later but, especially with a young kitten, the risk of a digestive disturbance will be minimized if you follow these guidelines, and do not change the cat's diet suddenly.

The journey home

Cats as a general rule do not like travelling, and need to be moved in a secure container. Although a young kitten may be transported sitting on a blanket on the knee of a passenger in a car, it will be safest for all concerned if a box is used.

Cheap, disposable cardboard containers can be purchased for this purpose, but tend not to be very satisfactory, certainly for adult cats. Their weight will displace the bottom of the box, and if they urinate during the journey, the saturated cardboard may collapse under their weight.

There is also a risk that by scratching at the sides, the cat may be able to force an exit through the roof of the box. This applies especially when ordinary cardboard boxes are used, where the flaps are simply folded in on each other.

The best option, bearing in mind that your kitten will inevitably need to be moved in the future, is to obtain a proper carrier. Wicker baskets of various designs are available, and those with a hinged lid are most suitable. If your cat is temperamental, and gets upset during a journey, it may be difficult to remove it from a basket with a door at its front. The cat is likely to retreat to the back, hissing and attempting to scratch when a hand is placed within to encourage it to come out of the basket.

Look carefully at the method of closing the cat basket. Plastic straps tend to weaken and break quite readily over a period of time.

Wire mesh carriers, coated in a washable epoxy resin, will not absorb urine in the same way as wicker baskets. The stress of travelling often causes a cat to defaecate and urinate, so that the basket must be easy to clean thoroughly. Place a thick layer of newspaper on the floor in any event, as this will help to absorb any seepage.

On top of the newspaper you can include an old piece of blanketing, which can be discarded if it becomes soiled, as the kitten may settle down here on the journey home.

Although a car provides the quickest means of travel, you can take a cat on public transport in most cases. Check beforehand though, and ensure that your cat is housed in a secure basket for the duration of the journey.

Right: *A wicker carrying basket. Be sure to line the base well with absorbent newspaper before putting the cat in it. The ties around the door must be properly secured or your cat may well escape.*

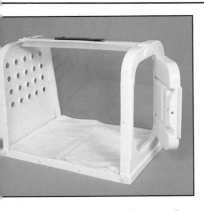

Above: *A secure carrying container will be essential whenever you move your cat.*

Above: *Many cats prefer to see where they are travelling. A see-through container is ideal.*

IN THE HOME

You will need to get some equipment before actually collecting your new cat, so a visit to your local pet store will be necessary, even if you obtain the kitten from another source. The largest selection of equipment is likely to be stocked by the bigger stores, but any particular requirements you have can usually be ordered for you by all pet stores.

Necessary equipment

Food and water bowls will be essential, and a wide variety of designs are likely to be encountered. Cats tend not to chew their bowls, unlike dogs, so that stout plastic containers can be provided. However, these may not prove very stable, and a heavier design is preferable.

For this reason the glazed ceramic pots sometimes marketed just as dog bowls are ideal for cats. These are easy to clean thoroughly and quite durable.

Stainless steel bowls can also be used, but these are probably easier to tip over than ceramic pots.

You will also need a brush to wash the food and water containers at least

Below: *A cardboard box can be converted into a useful temporary bed when lined with an old blanket.*

daily, plus a detergent for this purpose. Never include feeding containers used for cats in a bowl alongside human utensils. Cats tend to have an especially unpleasant range of bacteria as part of their normal mouth flora, and clearly, hygenic precautions should be taken when dealing with their food pots. Rinse these thoroughly after using the detergent to remove particles of uneaten food.

Another essential requirement for the newly-acquired cat or kitten will be a litter tray, and cat litter. Special plastic containers complete with a cover to prevent the contents being scattered over the floor are to be recommended. They can be lined, using newspaper or plastic sacks, and the litter applied on top, to facilitate cleaning.

Various types of cat litter are available, some of which will absorb odours. You will need sufficient to cover the floor of the tray to a depth of 2·5 cm (1 in) or so.

Most cats will accept litter very readily, but some owners prefer to provide peat, and garden soil. Yet these materials may well stain the fur and, once wet, are liable to be transferred from the cat's paws on to carpeting and surrounding furniture.

A plastic scoop may also be useful, in conjunction with the litter tray,

although it is probably easier to discard the whole contents of the tray once it has been used.

A bed is not an essential purchase from the outset, and indeed, you may prefer to use a cardboard box at first, with one of its sides cut down to permit access. The range of cat beds is surprisingly large, but a high price tag is no guarantee that it will ultimately appeal to your cat.

Remember when purchasing a bed that you will need to wash it at regular intervals, particularly during the warmer months of the year, since fleas will commonly breed in such surroundings. Ornate fabric designs therefore tend to be impractical, unless they are completely washable.

One option that cats appear to accept quite readily, both as a bed and play area, is a bean bag, available in various sizes, and usually equipped with removable covers. The contents of such bags are usually in the form of polystyrene granules, and they provide a cosy sleeping area, enabling the cat to curl into a ball, or lie out flat as it wishes.

Kittens in particular are playful by nature, and you will find a wide variety of toys to amuse them in the pet store. Again, concentrate on those which can be cleaned easily, and are relatively simple in their design. Balls are a particular favourite of many cats, but be sure that they cannot be swallowed accidentally, as this is liable to have fatal consequences.

You can obtain toys impregnated with the same chemical present in the plant called catnip *(Nepeta cataria)*, which most cats find highly appealing.

Some household objects can also be provided as playthings, such as empty cotton reels. Do not allow the cat to play with cotton itself though, because it may swallow this, or it may become caught around the cat's tongue with dire consequences.

Many cats enjoy stalking and pouncing on moving objects. A suitable length of thick rope can be obtained for this purpose.

Cats regularly exercise their claws, and while such games can assist in this regard, they may also resort to attacking furniture around the home.

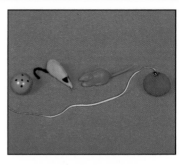

Above: *Many different toys are marketed for cats. Always check they are safe for your pet.*

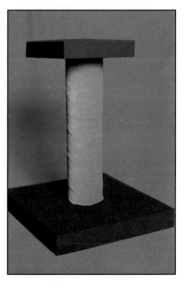

Above: *A scratching post can prove a useful investment, especially if your cat lives permanently indoors.*

Part of this behaviour may be traced to scent marking, for which purpose cats have glands between their toes.

Such behaviour may in fact be more common in older cats rather than kittens, and for those living indoors permanently, the provision of a suitable scratching post is to be recommended. You can purchase one of these, or alternatively make one using a thick branch of wood, set vertically on a solid base.

For longhaired cats in particular, you will need to acquire suitable grooming

instruments. It is a good idea to get a young kitten used to grooming right from the outset, so that it will not resent such treatment at a later stage. A variety of tools are available for this purpose.

A special flea comb will probably be essential, along with a broader-toothed grooming comb. Brushes will also be required, and these may have natural bristles or can be made of rubber, the latter type being favoured for shorthaired cats.

Depending on your circumstances, you may want to acquire a pen where the kitten can be confined for periods of the day. These come in sectional form, and the panels themselves should be covered with relatively fine mesh, so there is no risk of the kitten becoming caught up, trying to escape by this route.

Pens can be very useful when a kitten is being kept in a kitchen for example, with people regularly moving in and out for part of the day. There is then always the risk that it could slip out of the door undetected, if it was roaming free.

Early days
On its arrival home, the kitten or cat will probably be rather upset after the journey, and should be left alone to settle down, with dishes containing water, milk and food available in its

Above: *Establishing a routine for your kitten. Gentle grooming will help to remove moulted hair.*

new environment.

While you can let your new pet wander freely around the home, it will be better, at least initially, to restrict its domain. You will be able to supervise its movements more closely, so that accidents and resulting injuries involving the cat are less likely to arise.

The advantage of having a pen will be most apparent at this stage. Many owners choose to keep the kitten in the kitchen at first, but here the potential dangers are many, ranging from pans of boiling water to washing machines and dryers, with open fronts, which serve to attract cats.

If the kitten is confined to a pen for periods, it will be less likely to soil around the house, in a haphazard fashion, which can create serious problems later.

House-training should in fact begin as soon as possible; once you have obtained the kitten, ensure that the litter tray is freely accessible to it. Young cats should have trays with low sides, not exceeding 7.5 cm (3 in) in height, as otherwise they may be reluctant to enter the litter tray.

Having explored its new quarters, and probably eaten and drunk a little, the kitten is likely to want to use its

Above: *Your kitten will soon come to recognize its bed and will sleep here of its own accord. The bed needs to be easily washable.*

litter tray. Place it gently on the litter, and it should soon use it. After it has relieved itself, the kitten will probably then go to sleep.

Care needs to be taken when introducing the young cat to other members of the household. Children will naturally be very curious, and the kitten's every move is likely to be watched closely. If the children are not used to cats, explain to them how they can help with its care, including feeding and grooming, but do not encourage them to pick up the cat on their own, since they may end up being badly scratched or even bitten. A period of adjustment will also be required for existing pets.

Dogs usually prove reasonably tolerant towards a young kitten or even an older cat, but it can be a different proposition with other cats already present in the household. At first, keep them apart, until the new arrival is settled, and then cautiously introduce them, without precipitating a conflict by placing one directly alongside the other.

Allow them to come to terms with each other, taking care to reinforce your bond with the established pet by giving it plenty of affection, in the face of the newcomer.

An older cat will naturally tend to dominate a kitten, and acquiring another adult cat is more likely to cause conflict, with the dominance of the original cat being potentially threatened by the newcomer. Do not expect the situation to be resolved in a short space of time: it will be a gradual process, and the cats may be noticeably wary of each other for several months. Direct conflict is less

Below: *Integrating the kitten alongside other pets. Some dogs will form close bonds with cats.*

Above: *Most cats prefer canned or fresh-cooked foods, but dried diets can be valuable.*

likely to occur, however, as time elapses, and the hierarchy between the individuals is established.

Feeding

A kitten will grow quite fast, and this will be reflected in its appetite. Indeed, at the age of seven weeks, it may be consuming the equivalent of 20 per cent of its body weight each day.

In the past, when fresh meat and offal were widely used for feeding cats, nutritional shortcomings could often be seen. Now, as a result of intensive study of their requirements, you can obtain a variety of complete

Below: *Providing a varied diet from the outset will help to prevent fussy feeding habits later in life.*

diets for your pets. These offer all the necessary ingredients, in the correct proportions, to keep your pet in good condition.

For a young kitten, therefore, you should obtain one of the canned foods offering a complete diet for young, growing cats, assuming this is what it was offered through the weaning phase. If this was not so, you will need to introduce the canned food gradually.

It can be useful to offer other forms of complete food on occasions as the kitten grows up. This should help to ensure that it will take such items readily, although cats do show a preference for certain foods rather than others, and a few individuals may prove rather fussy eaters.

Fresh meats and fish

Some owners prefer to offer freshly cooked foods. Although these are usually highly palatable, they do not contain all the essential elements needed to maintain a cat, especially a kitten, in top condition.

Meat such as steak, for example, is deficient in certain respects, notably in terms of its calcium/phosphorus ratio (where there is a wide imbalance in favour of phosphorus) and Vitamin A. While liver is a valuable source of this vitamin, offal generally is low in calcium, although milk may help to counter any calcium deficiency in the diet. Variety, therefore, is important with fresh foods.

You can use a vitamin and mineral supplement, in powdered form, to counter any imbalances. This is simply sprinkled over the cat's food. Such products will not be required if the cat is being fed a balanced, complete diet however, since these ingredients will be present at the correct levels.

Excessive use of such supplements should be avoided in any event, since they are liable to have adverse effects. Instructions can be found on the packaging, and within these limits the supplements will prove beneficial.

Never feed individual fresh foods on a regular basis, but rotate them if they are to form the mainstay of the cat's diet. Be aware of the nutritional shortcomings of each type of meat. Although pig's lungs, sold as 'lights', are readily eaten by cats, these are low in protein, and need to be cut into pieces for most cats.

Fresh food should always be cooked thoroughly, because of the slight risk of transmitting either bacteria or parasites to your cat. Do not provide hot food though, as it may burn the cat's mouth.

Fish in particular is best cooked, because certain types contain an enzyme known as thiaminase, which destroys Vitamin B_1 present in the diet, creating a deficiency. This is likely to cause a depression of appetite, and the cat becomes progressively duller; if this not corrected, fits will then be seen, followed by death. When cooked however, the enzyme in the fish is inactivated.

Another important point to check with fish is that it is properly filleted. Fish bones are potentially lethal for cats, as they may cause an obstruction if swallowed.

The oil present in certain kinds of fish is also hazardous, if these form the basis of the cat's diet. Over a period of time, the condition known as yellow fat disease (or pansteatitis) because of the characteristic alteration in colour to the body's fat stores, is likely to arise. This is a painful condition, and the cat will almost certainly show displeasure at being touched or restrained in any way.

Another typical sign of pansteatitis is clumsiness, and indeed, a cat which is thought to have behavioural problems could in fact be affected with this ailment. The condition is most likely to arise in younger individuals, and obviously treatment will entail modifying the diet. Vitamin E supplementation is also usually recommended, since cats suffering from yellow fat disease tend to be deficient in this vitamin as well.

Other important nutritional diseases in cats do in fact stem from overdosage with certain vitamins, notably those of the fat-soluble group, which comprise Vitamins A, D, E and K. These are actually stored in the body, in the liver. Administration of cod-liver oil as a tonic needs to be carried out carefully therefore, because although a valuable source of such vitamins, an excess over a period of time will inevitably be harmful.

This can be exacerbated by the cat's food. For example, a diet containing both liver and cod-liver oil is likely to precipitate the disease known as hypervitaminosis A, since both items are sources of vitamin A.

YOUR CAT'S DIET

KITTEN	Meals per day	Amount
Weaning (8 weeks) to 3 months	4-6	
4-5 months	4-5	80-190g/3-6oz
6 months	3-4	275g/9oz
7-8 months	3	370g/12oz
		370g/12oz
ADULT		
9 months & over	2-3	
		400g/14oz

Fresh water should always be available for your cat or kitten to drink at will.

This condition will adversely affect the growth of the forelegs, and is also likely to cause malformation of the vertebral column. One of the early signs will be a stiff gait, and again, the cat will not like being handled, because this will be painful.

Kittens are most at risk from nutritional shortcomings in their diet, as a result of their rapid growth rate. Skeletal abnormalities are almost inevitable if they are fed on a diet of offal and meat alone, because of the relative shortage of calcium in these foodstuffs.

The body's reserves of calcium are concentrated in the skeletal system, but it is potentially dangerous to feed your cat with bones, especially from chicken carcasses which are relatively fragile and splinter readily. As a result, the addition of a sprinkling of *sterilized* bone meal to the cat's food is recommended. Dairy products, notably cheese, are also valuable for their calcium content.

Above: *These Oriental tabbies are sharing their food, but generally it is better to feed cats separately.*

The cat's nutritional needs

As a hunter a cat will tend to eat the whole carcass of its prey, such as mice, and thus will not develop such deficiencies. Cats must be fed meat or fish (they are known as obligate carnivores) and will not survive on a vegetarian diet, because of their specific nutritional requirements.

The constituents of protein, known as amino acid residues, are individually significant, and the cat is unable to synthesize certain of these in its body. Such essential amino acids are not present in vegetable protein, and thus need to be included as part of the cat's diet in the form of protein of animal origin.

For this reason, you cannot use dog food, since this tends to be deficient in certain vital respects for cats. The shortage of the amino acid taurine will ultimately affect the cat's vision, and cats also need a relatively high level of fat in their diet, which may not be adequate in all dog foods.

Dog foods contain carbohydrates, but these are usually unimportant in the diet of a cat, since this food element is not present in bulk in animal tissues. Sources of carbohydrate,

such as cooked rice and bread, may however occasionally be eaten by cats in domestic surroundings.

Prepared cat foods

Canned foods are more palatable than other prepared foodstuffs for most cats. These have a high moisture content, averaging perhaps 80 per cent, and are available in various flavours. It can be useful to alternate the flavours in a range so as to provide the cat with some variety, if it is kept on a diet of canned food alone.

Do not confuse these flavoured varieties, which also contain all the necessary vitamins and minerals, providing a balanced diet, with plain brands, which contain just fish or plain meat. These foods can be useful as occasional treats, but cannot be relied upon to meet the cat's nutritional requirements.

As a guide, the average consumption of an adult cat being kept on a canned diet is likely to be around two-thirds of the average 400 g (14 oz) can daily. If in any doubt, check the labelling carefully, so you will know if you are purchasing a complete diet.

Do not offer more than your cat is likely to eat at any time, especially with canned foods. These tend to dry up, becoming less palatable as a result, and will also attract flies in warm weather. Indeed, it is preferable to train your cat to have specific feeding times from the outset.

A young kitten will need probably

three or four meals a day, and this can be reduced to two, morning and evening, once the cat is about nine months old. Unlike their wild counterparts however, domestic cats will not necessarily eat all the food offered in one short session, but usually return several times to the feeding bowl. Clearly, the feeding routine will be influenced by your own lifestyle.

When offering either canned or fresh cooked foods be sure to cut them into small pieces, and place the feeding bowl on a surface where any spillage can be easily cleaned up. Large chunks of food are liable to be pulled out of the bowl, and may even be dragged across a carpet by the cat. A deep feeding container will tend to encourage this behaviour, which simply reflects the cat's desire to chew the food into a more manageable size before swallowing it.

Once a can is opened it should be kept in a refrigerator if possible, so that the contents will remain fresh for several days. It is best to transfer the food to a clean plastic container with a sealable lid, rather than leaving it in the can. Similarly, freshly cooked foods should also be refrigerated after they have cooled.

While cans have been the most popular form of prepared food for cats for a long period, there has recently been rapid growth in the semi-moist sector of the market. Such foods, as their name suggests, have a lower moisture content than canned diets, and are sold in packeted form. As such, they are lighter and more convenient than cans, and the food itself is sealed in individual sachets.

These foods tend to be somewhat less palatable than canned rations, however, although they are designed in such a way as to have maximum appeal to the cat's owner. The appearance of such foods tends to be both meaty and succulent, but not all cats are so enthusiastic about this type of food. Dried diets contain even less water than these semi-moist foods, typically less than 10 per cent. They can therefore be provided throughout the day, without any risk of deterioration. It

is important that you provide adequate fluid for your cat to drink to compensate for the relative shortage resulting from their food.

Some urinary problems have been linked to the use of dried diets, most notably feline urological syndrome (FUS) (see page 93). Cats which have previously been affected by this problem or have a history of urinary diseases should not be given dried food on a regular basis.

Feeding guidelines
Obesity is not a widespread problem in cats, possibly because they show no particular fondness for carbohydrate, but if you see that your cat is becoming obese, you should start to ration its food intake. Do not leave dried food constantly available therefore, only offering the recommended amount each day.

Conversely, if your cat does not appear to be eating as much as usual, this may be a sign of illness. Alternatively, it may be receiving food elsewhere (from a neighbour, for example) if it is allowed to roam freely.

Cats are actually quite fastidious about their food, and may ignore fresh food provided in a dirty bowl. Always wash the food container after each meal if the cat is being offered perishable foodstuffs, and certainly change the contents of the bowl at least twice a week if you are using dry food.

Follow the feeding guidelines with dry foods, as they will give a good indication of the quantity your cat should be eating. If you want to keep a check on its food intake, weigh your cat regularly. This is most easily accomplished by standing on scales, holding your pet. Note the figure, and then subtract your weight from this combined total.

A figure much over 5kg (11 lb) tends to indicate the onset of obesity, which is more likely to arise in neutered animals. Queens as a rule are generally lighter than toms, rarely weighing more than 4 kg (9 lb).

Most kittens will continue growing for the first year, and a steady increase in their weight should be apparent over this period. Typical signs of

underfeeding are likely to include protruding ribs, and weight loss elsewhere, often most noticeable around the head. It can be more difficult to recognize these changes in longhaired cats, although the appearance of their coat is likely to suffer accordingly.

Water and milk
The fluid intake of your cat will vary, depending on its diet, and also its environment. Clearly, it is likely to drink more during warm weather, and when eating dried food. It is of course difficult to assess your cat's drinking habits in any event, since if it is allowed outside, it may well drink from puddles, and even garden ponds.

Some cats will drink from a dripping tap, pawing at the falling water droplets. Do ensure that they cannot have access to a toilet however, certainly if there is any risk of bleach being present in solution here, as this will prove toxic.

Try to monitor the fluid intake though, especially if your cat is being fed on a dried diet. In the wild, cats do not need to drink a great deal , as they obtain much of their fluid requirement from their food.

Some cats are reluctant to make up the shortfall resulting from dried food, but certainly if inadequate water is provided, then the likelihood of urinary tract problems is increased considerably, particularly in male cats. Always ensure that your cat has access to a clean bowl of water therefore, irrespective of whether or not you are offering milk.

In theory, there is really no need to provide milk for your cat, although the cat will invariably drink it readily. The major constituent of milk is water, but two other ingredients are of significance. Some cats, notably Siamese and related breeds, appear to be unable to accept cow's milk in particular, which gives them severe diarrhoea. It may be that they are allergic to some of the proteins present in cows' milk, and they may also lack the necessary enzyme to digest the milk sugar, or lactose.

While milk can be offered regularly to those cats which show no adverse effects from consuming it, you should not attempt to provide milk in place of water. Milk can also sour quite readily in warm weather, when not refrigerated, so provide only a small volume at any time, and wash the container thoroughly, using a detergent, soon afterwards.

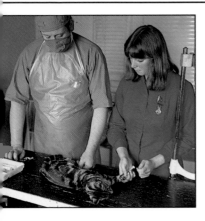

Above: *Veterinarians can be found without difficulty. Emergency care is always available when needed.*

Left: *Healthy cats look forward to their food, and they should be encouraged to eat a varied diet.*

Visiting a veterinarian

Soon after obtaining your cat, you will need to visit a veterinarian. In general, it is best to choose a veterinarian near to where you live, so that in an emergency you can reach the surgery without difficulty. A number of veterinary practices can be found in most major towns, as a glance at the yellow pages or a telephone book will confirm.

You may of course already have visited a veterinarian nearby, or a friend may have recommended a practice to you. The choice is not too difficult, since the training of all veterinarians is both broad and thorough, so that they will all be well acquainted with feline problems.

Costs do vary, and in the first instance you may want to check on the cost of inoculations. The fees charged are difficult to compare, because the overheads of some practices are higher than others, and their standard of equipment could be superior. It may be worth continuing with the practice which administered the first set of inoculations to your kitten, if this is based nearby. Indeed, breeders will usually be able to recommend a veterinarian if you have any doubts.

Many practices today are comprised of groups of veterinarians, who operate on a rota system. While for routine treatment, such as a course of inoculations, this is of no real significance, you may prefer to see one veterinarian if your cat falls ill. Find out whether you will be able to do so on your first visit.

Some practices have an appointments system, whereas others operate at least some surgeries on an open basis, so that you can just turn up, and wait in turn to see the veterinarian. You should contact the practice in advance to enquire whether it will be necessary to make an appointment, and you will be able to find out the times of the surgeries in any event.

While all practices try to keep to their appointments system, emergencies do arise and may cause delays, which should not reflect badly on the veterinarian and staff concerned. If your cat needed immediate treatment, you would not be happy to be told that there were appointment cases waiting which would have to be seen first!

Inoculations

It is now possible to protect your cat against most of the serious viral diseases which formerly claimed the lives of many cats annually. The vaccines used confer a very high degree of protection, and have no adverse side-effects in the vast majority of cases. Regular 'booster' inoculations will be required annually, but if you suspect that your cat may be pregnant by this stage, do inform your veterinarian, since this is likely to affect the choice of vaccine.

As a general guide, a young kitten will require two sets of inoculations, administered first at about nine weeks of age, and then three weeks later. This ensures that the kitten should be fully protected against the killer diseases concerned.

After birth, the young kitten receives antibodies (protection against infection) via its mother's milk, but as weaning approaches, so the level of antibodies declines. At this stage, the kitten's own immune system starts to become effective.

Yet if the maternal antibodies are still present when the first inoculation is given, they will prevent the vaccine from stimulating the kitten's own body defences.

Other kittens will have no maternal antibodies left by the age of nine weeks, so for them the first inoculation will be successful.

At the age of three months, none of the young cats possess any maternal antibodies, so the second inoculation is given at this stage to ensure protection for them all.

It is usual to give vaccines for feline infectious enteritis, as well as respiratory disease viruses, including feline calicivirus, which cause 'cat flu'. Your young cat will not be able to go outside until it has completed these initial inoculations, and should be kept away from other cats in the interim. In the veterinarian's waiting room, therefore, ensure that the kitten remains within its basket, and is not allowed to walk around the floor.

If you intend to keep your cat indoors permanently, it is still sensible to take advantage of the protection provided by inoculations, as at a later stage it may have to mix with other cats, at a cattery, for example. A set of inoculations will almost certainly be compulsory for cats admitted to such establishments, even at short notice, so it is also important to keep your record card safely.

This can be used as evidence of the inoculations being given, after it has been signed by your veterinarian, and should also tell you when boosters need to be given.

Depending on the part of the world where you are living, your cat may also require a rabies vaccination. In Britain, Ireland and Australia, where this dreaded viral disease does not at present occur, this inoculation is not administered routinely. Elsewhere, check with your veterinarian: in some areas, rabies inoculations are compulsory, although it is possible that the situation in this regard may change from time to time.

A major breakthrough against another viral disease of cats has seen the launch of a vaccine to combat feline leukaemia virus (FeLV) in the United States. First used during 1985, this vaccine does not yet offer full protection to all members of a susceptible population of cats, but tests suggest that it is about 80 per cent effective.

Since studies have revealed that 1·5 million cats are affected annually with this disease in the United States alone, and approximately two-thirds will ultimately die as a result of contracting it, the vaccine is a worthwhile means of reducing this death toll quite considerably. Further work is continuing to improve its efficacy, and in time it will probably become more widely available.

There is often no need to be present when your cat is given the vaccines, since the veterinarian will probably have a member of staff on hand, assisting in the surgery. If you are squeamish, it is far better to explain and step outside at this stage, rather than fainting during the proceedings!

A surprisingly large number of people dislike seeing their cat inoculated, so there is no need to feel embarrassed. Indeed, on occasions it may be better to have a skilled assistant restraining your cat, as a few individuals prove very difficult to handle after the journey to the surgery.

Perhaps not surprisingly, Siamese tend to be the worst offenders in this regard, hissing and spitting before they are even removed from their carrying container.

Vaccines are normally administered either just below the skin at the scruff of the neck, or into the muscle of the hind leg, which may cause the cat slightly more discomfort, although this will not last long. In the case of some vaccines protecting against respiratory disease, these are given intra-nasally — they are actually squirted up the nostrils. The cat may sneeze soon after the procedure has been carried out, but this should not however interfere with the action of the vaccine.

Deworming
On your first visit to the veterinarian, you will also need to ask for advice on deworming, especially with a young kitten which is likely to be badly

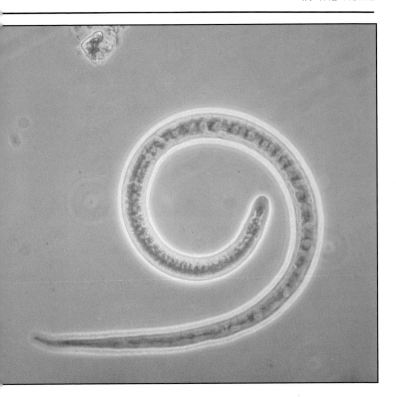

infected with such parasites. It may well have obtained a fairly heavy burden from its mother, especially if she was not treated regularly.

This often happens with ascarid worms, which are members of the roundworm group. These have a specialized life cycle which entails migrating out of the intestine (where they developed) into the body of the cat during their immature stage. They lie dormant in the body tissue until, if their host is a female cat, she begins to produce milk for kittens; they then come to life and migrate via the mammary glands to the young kittens when they suckle.

Here, in the intestines of the young cats, the larvae develop in the usual way, producing eggs which are then voided from the body in faeces.

The effects of these parasites are quite variable in kittens. They may cause diarrhoea, vomiting and pot-bellied appearance. Treatment from an early age is therefore to be recommended.

Above: Roundworms are common feline parasites, differing from tapeworms, which are ribbon-like.

In most cases, this begins when the kittens are about three weeks of age, and is repeated at similar intervals for a period of about six months. Subsequently, deworming twice a year should be adequate to counter these roundworms.

In the older cat, tapeworms are likely to assume greater significance, especially in the case of cats which hunt, since these parasites pass through an intermediate host, such as a mouse, rather than infecting the cat directly. Fleas can also transmit tapeworms, so treatment for them should also be discussed with your veterinarian at an early stage.

While stray cats are most likely to be in need of medication for tapeworms, all cats should be started on a course of treatment from the age of about six months onwards. This will need to be repeated twice a year, particularly if

Above: *Cats are fastidious creatures, and many spend long periods grooming themselves.*

Left: *Daily grooming is essential. Here this longhair is being carefully combed by its owner.*

your cat spends part of its time outside.

If you have any specific worries about your cat or kitten, do not be afraid to mention them when you first visit the veterinarian. Your pet will be given a routine examination prior to being given its inoculations, but you should warn the veterinarian if you believe that the kitten is ill in any way.

Coat care
One of the common behavioural traits observed in domestic cats is grooming. They will spend long periods attending to their coat, using both their tongue and paws for this purpose. This helps to keep the coat in good condition, and also appears to have a social function, since cats do groom each other on occasions.

In spite of their grooming activities, however, cats must have their coats combed and brushed daily or as appropriate by their owners. The only exceptions to this rule are the Rexes

and the Sphynx, which simply do not have enough hair.

The method of grooming depends on the breed concerned and must take into account its coat type. Cats without a dense undercoat, including the Siamese and British Shorthair breeds, should be brushed so as to raise the fur from its natural positioning. It can then be combed, and loose hairs will accumulate between the teeth of the comb.

More careful grooming, following the same basic pattern, is required for cats which have a thick undercoat. The Russian Blue and Abyssinian are typical examples in this category.

Perhaps not surprisingly, coat care for longhaired cats is rather more complex. A comb is used around the eyes, while the ruff around the face needs to be highlighted - and a brush will be useful for this purpose. It is usual to groom the body with a comb, directing the hair vertically, and then brushing it back.

Failure to groom a longhaired cat regularly will lead to its fur becoming matted, and, perhaps more significantly, it will almost certainly suffer from hair-balls. As the cat grooms itself, using its tongue, some of its loose hairs accumulate on the roughened surface there.

Since the papillae responsible are directed backwards, the cat tends to swallow the loose fur, rather than being able to spit it out of its mouth. The hairs will coalesce over a period of time in the digestive tract, causing an obstruction in the cat's stomach.

A typical sign of the presence of a hair-ball is when the cat appears to want to eat, but actually consumes very little, although in other respects it seems quite healthy. It may also try to vomit in an attempt to remove the mass of hair.

In severe cases, administration of about 5ml (1 teaspoon) of liquid paraffin either given directly or on the

BASIC GROOMING EQUIPMENT

1 Dual-purpose bristle and wire brushes for general grooming. Care should be taken when using the wire side, as hard brushing can strip the coat.
2 Pure bristle brush, with short, soft bristles, especially good for shorthaired cats.
3 Rubber brush with short flexible filaments, and rigid plastic type for general grooming.
4 Blunt-ended scissors for cutting through mats (in a longhaired coat).
5 Toothbrush for brushing up the coat of a longhaired cat around the ears and eyes.
6 Cotton-wool buds for cleaning the outer parts of ears.
7 Wide, flat tail comb ensures each hair on the tail of a long-haired cat is separate. Also known as a slicker brush.

8 Specially shaped scissors for trimming the claws.
9 Fine-toothed comb for short-haired cats - smooths the coat and removes fleas and dirt.
10 Wide-toothed comb for removing tangles in the fur of longhaired cats.
11 Metal dual-purpose comb with wide- and medium-spaced teeth, ideal as general purpose groomer.
12 Non-toxic baby shampoo.
13 Bay rum spirit conditioner; removes grease from the coat.
14 Surgical spirit essential for re-moving stains from pale coats.
15 Cotton wool for cleansing eyes, ears and nose.
16 Non-toxic grooming powder or baby powder gives body to the coat. Sprinkle into the fur and brush out completely.

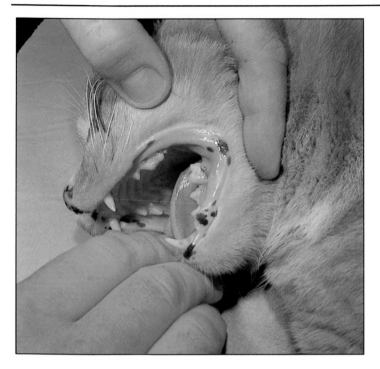

Above: *Check your cat's teeth occasionally. They can be cleaned with damp cotton-wool.*

cat's food if it is eating, should act as an effective lubricant, assisting the passage of the fur ball through the digestive tract. You can also use a commercial hair-ball remedy which is a combination of emulsified petroleum jelly flavoured with malt or other palatable tastes. Most cats will lick it off a spoon.

The teeth
When grooming a longhaired cat, pay particular attention also to the hair around the jaws. This can easily become matted and soiled with food, giving rise to localized skin infections, as well as creating a bad odour here. The cat's teeth will also need to be inspected on occasions, certainly if you can detect bad breath, or if it appears to be having difficulty eating.

Cat's teeth do not decay to the same extent as those of humans, but they are more likely to suffer from accumulations of plaque or tartar. This is usually most common in cats being fed on wet-type foods, as dry diets help to prevent the build-up of tartar.

Tartar in its early stage forms yellowish-grey deposits on the sides of the teeth. This may spread, extending to the gums. Here, inflammation called gingivitis follows, with the part of the gum affected becoming deep red in colour. It will become eroded in time, and then the root of the tooth will be weakened and exposed to infection.

Older cats are most at risk from such accumulations of tartar, and once deposits are apparent, make an appointment for your veterinarian to remove the tartar, which is a combination of salts precipitated from saliva, food particles and bacteria.

Brushing the cat's teeth regularly is not usually recommended; certainly do not use toothpaste, which is resented by most cats. It is better to wipe the teeth carefully, using damp cotton-wool well moistened with a solution of hydrogen peroxide. Toothbrushes are severe on the cat's gums, and it will be reluctant to allow

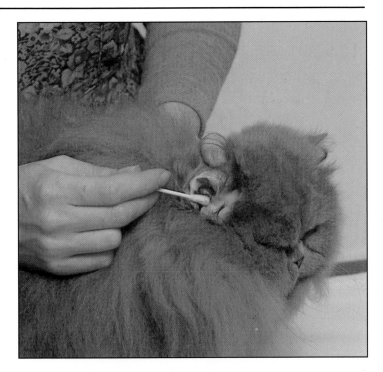

you to repeat the treatment.

You should accustom a young kitten to having its mouth opened from the outset, even though this will not be strictly necessary. In later life, however, it should be much easier to dose the cat with tablets, or indeed clean its teeth as required. Expect to find teeth around the home once your kitten is about six months. By this stage it will be replacing its first, deciduous set of teeth, starting with the small incisors at the front of the mouth and working round via the canines to the larger premolars.

When it is teething, you are likely to find that the kitten is more destructive, gnawing at toys and perhaps furniture. This eases the discomfort during this phase, and although it can be difficult if the home is damaged, the problem should ultimately resolve itself. You can try offering a hide chew, available from most pet stores, as a suitable target for the cat's erupting teeth.

The ears
Besides checking the mouth when grooming your cat, you should also

Above: *Wax may accumulate in the ear canal. Careful cleaning is possible with a cotton-wool bud.*

look carefully at the ears for any sign of dirt within the ear canal. Some individuals produce more wax than others, and Rexes especially will probably need their ears cleaned quite regularly. If the cat is seen scratching or pawing at its ears this may indicate that it has ear mites, which can cause considerable irritation, and veterinary treatment will be required.

For routine cleaning, the use of a damp cotton wool bud is to be recommended, with the cat positioned on a level surface, such as a table. The folds within the ear should be wiped carefully, ensuring that the debris can be removed.

In bad cases, you may need to use cotton wool moistened with olive oil which will serve to break down any stubborn deposits in the canal. Under no circumstances, especially with a bud, should you push right into the ear, as this will be painful, and certainly could damage the cat's hearing.

47

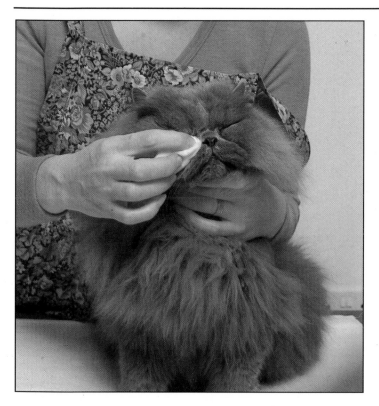

Above: *Any discharge from the eyes will stain the surrounding fur, and should be wiped off.*

The eyes

The eyes in contrast rarely need attention, although in a few breeds, notably the Peke-face, which has a compressed face resembling that of a Pekingese dog, there may be deposits of tear fluid on the fur around the lower eyelid. This is because the tear ducts, which normally drain the fluid from the eyes, are affected by the flattening of the face in this breed, and do not function properly.

Longhaired cats sometimes have dirt visible at the corner of the eyes closest to the nose, and this can also develop to form trails of fluid. It should be possible to wipe this away carefully, using cotton wool moistened with water, but if the cat appears to have difficulty in keeping its eyes open, this could be indicative of a more serious problem, such as respiratory infection.

The claws

You should also inspect your cat's claws occasionally, especially if it appears to be having difficulty in freeing itself from material and bedding. You may find that the sharp points of the claws have become slightly overgrown. This is most likely in cats which spend all of their time indoors, and have little opportunity to keep their claws in trim, by climbing, for example.

It is probably best to ask your veterinarian for advice and assistance if you suspect that the claws are overgrown. Bear in mind that those on the hind feet are normally shorter than the claws on the front feet.

You can cut them yourself, providing that you have a suitable implement for the task. Scissors are not adequate for this purpose, since they are liable to split the claw, rather than cutting through it cleanly. Obtain a pair of bone clippers or special clippers for trimming which can be

Cat Eyes

Pg. 48

relied upon to snip off the overgrown ends completely.

You will probably need assistance when cutting the claws, with someone else restraining the cat. The paw should be held carefully, so that the claw to be cut is clearly evident.

The task will be much easier if your cat has pale claws, since you will then be able to see the blood supply as a darker red streak, disappearing some distance down the claw. Make your cut a short distance clear of the point where the red line disappears, and this should cause the cat no pain, nor will there be any bleeding. If, however, you do misjudge the cut, apply a styptic pencil to the bleeding tip.

There is no point in clipping a cat's claws with a view to stopping it scratching furniture. The cat should be persuaded to use its scratching post instead when it attempts to scratch elsewhere around the home. In order to encourage a reluctant individual to investigate a scratching post, you can

Above: *If your cat's claws get too long or curl round they will need to be cut back with sharp clippers.*

Below: *Take care not to cut into the quick of the claw, as this will be painful and cause bleeding.*

TRIMMING CLAWS

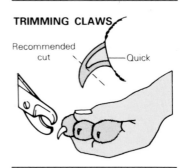

scent the site with catmint, hanging an impregnated toy over it, for example. The cat will start to paw at it here, and

should soon use the post for its intended purpose.

The operation known as onychectomy is a barbaric solution, rarely favoured by veterinarians or cat breeders, entailing the removal of all the cat's claws. You will have difficulty in finding any veterinarian willing to undertake such surgery. In addition, cats which have been declawed cannot be exhibited, and will inevitably be at a distinct disadvantage if they are allowed outside.

Other behavioural problems
Certain traits which are apparent in young kittens may develop into serious problems once the cat is older unless they are corrected at an early age. Some kittens may scratch and even bite when they are being played with, and this behaviour is liable to create difficulties in a home, especially alongside young children.

When a kitten reacts in this way in the course of a game, be firm with it. Pick it up, and place it in another part of the room. Then ignore the kitten for a period if it returns to you. Only as a last

Above: *Cats use their claws in everyday situations, and declawing cannot be recommended.*

resort should you give it a gentle slap on its hindquarters. A spray of water can prove an equally effective deterrent.

Another problem which first becomes apparent during kittenhood is wool-sucking. The young cat will toy with material in its mouth, and ultimately may swallow some of the fibres. The precise cause is unclear, but it is known that this condition is more common in pedigree cats.

Try to discourage the habit by not using woollen bedding materials, and by playing with your kitten for longer periods. It should then be more inclined to sleep, instead of sitting and playing with wool. Modifications to the diet may also prove valuable in some cases; you can try increasing the level of fibre by mixing bran in with canned food.

Some cats will prove troublesome by climbing around the room, and possibly up people's legs as well. This

Above: *Cats will normally bury their faeces, digging a shallow hollow in loose soil beforehand.*

Below: *A litter tray with cat litter. A plastic liner at the base of the tray makes cleaning easier.*

will be painful, and such behaviour should be firmly discouraged, in a similar way to that recommended for cats which scratch during a game. It can be much harder to prevent a cat from jumping on to furniture, especially as cats are tree-climbers by nature.

Encourage the cat to take more exercise out of doors if possible, or alternatively increase the period of time which you spend playing with it.

This should again serve to tire it out, so that it will be less enthusiastic about displaying its athletic prowess around the home.

Remember that if a cat is frightened it is likely to seek a higher vantage point, and should two cats that are not well acquainted be housed in the same room, they may both try to climb as high as possible, damaging ornaments in the process.

House-training
The most serious behavioural problem is likely to arise if the cat is not trained to use its litter box regularly, right from the outset. Remember that kittens will almost certainly need to have access to a litter tray soon after a meal.

Cats are relatively easy to house-train successfully because they are naturally clean animals. Always place the kitten on the litter after each meal, and you should soon find that it returns there automatically. If it refuses to use the litter tray, it may well be because you have not emptied soiled litter. Kittens will often ignore a contaminated litter tray, preferring to find a new locality.

If an accident does occur, there is little point in getting angry with the kitten. Grab the litter tray and transfer the kitten to it if it is caught in the act. A litter tray which has sides that are too high may be ignored by a kitten.

House-training should become easier once the kitten has completed its inoculations, and can be let outside to attend to its toilet functions. The odour of cat urine can be especially pungent around the home, and thorough cleaning afterwards will be required.

It is best if the removal of cat faeces is not undertaken by pregnant women, because of the slight risk of contracting the protozoal disease toxoplasmosis (see page 88). This can result occasionally in miscarriage, if the woman has had no previous exposure to this disease.

A much greater risk of this infection for humans is from raw meat, and this is one reason why only cooked foods should be offered to cats, in order to limit the possible spread of this and other infections.

OUT OF DOORS

Even if you obtain an adult cat, which has been fully vaccinated, it is not advisable to let it outside into a garden shortly after bringing it home. The cat is liable to stray and, especially if it came from a nearby locality, it may well attempt to return to its former home. You will therefore need to keep your new pet indoors for at least a fortnight.

Most tales about how to train your cat to return home, such as smearing its paws with butter, have no real factual basis, and are not likely to be effective.

Do not force your cat, or indeed a kitten, once its course of inoculations has been completed, to go outside. Let them explore as they wish. You can leave the door open, and encourage your new pet to follow you, by calling it. The cat should be showing clear signs of recognizing its name by this stage. If you obtain an adult cat

however, it can be unwise to alter its name, since it will be much slower to respond following its rechristening.

Once the cat has ventured forth, spend time with it in the garden. Most kittens, and indeed older cats, will sniff cautiously around their new environment, and are generally unlikely to wander far at this stage. Indeed, they may well follow you, to the extent of going back indoors at the same time. Gradually, however, their confidence will grow, and they will integrate into the feline population in your area.

Do take care from this point onwards to ensure that queens are adequately protected against having unwanted litters, once they are about five months old. Even if you plan to breed from your cat at a later date, it is best not to let her mate at the earliest opportunity.

Cat flaps
In order to allow your cat to come and go at will, you may decide to obtain a cat flap. This is usually fitted on to an

Below: *Cats will soon learn to use a cat-flap, although some initial training will probably be needed.*

exterior door leading into the garden, although it may be attached to a wall if necessary. This is likely to prove more difficult, and could be draughty.

For this reason, some cat owners with conservatories prefer to have the cat flap fitted to the exterior door of the conservatory, rather than the house itself. The cat can then come into a snug bed, but the use of a cat flap will not cause you any major problems in the house.

A drawback of many designs of cat flap is that you actually have no control over which cats come into your home. You may be unfortunate enough to have an intact tom attracted inside, which then proceeds to spray carpets and furniture with urine in characteristic fashion.

This can be overcome to some extent by fitting your cat with a special collar, which incorporates a magnet. This will serve to operate the door when the cat approaches, but in practice others may still gain access at the same time.

The design of the cat flap itself may also help in this respect, since some can be opened only from inside. You will have to teach your cat to operate the door in the first instance, although cats rapidly learn the technique.

Be sure to position the bottom of the flap about 10 cm (4 in) off the ground, so that the cat can get in and out without difficulty. Although you could make these flaps yourself, it is probably best to obtain one of the commercially-available designs. Large cat flaps are not to be recommended, since these are likely to prove draughty, and children may even be tempted to get through the opening, sometimes becoming stuck in the process.

If you opt for a hinged flap, raise the flap at first so that there is an opening, fixing the flap firmly above so it cannot fall down on to the cat. Should the flap hit the cat, it will be less keen to use the opening, especially when this is an unfamiliar means of access.

Place the cat on the inside, and go round to the outside with a titbit, such as a piece of chicken, or other fresh meat. Keeping the outside door closed, call the cat to you, staying close to the flap if it is reluctant to emerge. Most cats will readily go through the opening, however, especially if they are then rewarded with a titbit.

Repeat the procedure, in the reverse direction. Then lower the flap slightly, propping it ajar with a branch or similar light piece of wood. Now, when you call the cat, it should use its front paw to lift the flap further, allowing it to get out. By this stage, the cat will have grown used to the flap, and soon you should be able to let the flap hang in its correct position, as your

CAT FLAPS

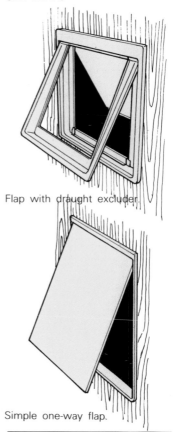

Flap with draught excluder.

Simple one-way flap.

Above: *Two designs of cat-flap. The cat will have to use its paw to gain access in some cases.*

pet starts to go in and out without any hesitation.

It will be better to obtain a flap which incorporates a draught excluder, rather than one which is simply hinged. A slightly different type of cat flap has a circular rather than square opening, with pieces of plastic or rubber forming the interior. The cat simply pushes through these as it moves back and forth. It is best to remove one or two of these components when training the cat to use this form of entrance, so that a gap will be clearly apparent at first.

Collars

Although a collar will be essential in conjunction with certain types of cat flap, not all owners are keen to fit their cats with collars. This applies particularly to those cats which are great climbers, since they could become caught up by their collar on a branch. A slow death from strangulation is then likely, as the cat struggles to free itself.

Yet a cat wearing a collar can carry an identification capsule, containing details of its home written on a piece of paper within. There are times when this information could be important, if the cat strays, or becomes injured in a road traffic accident.

In addition, a bell can also be fitted to the collar, helping to warn birds of the presence of the cat, so it should be less likely to catch them.

If you opt to equip your cat with a collar, be sure to obtain one which is elasticated. This should ensure that if the cat does become caught accidentally by its collar, this will not tighten around the neck, but expand, leaving the cat able to wriggle free.

As an additional precaution, you may like to cut the collar, and stitch in self-opening material, which, when pulled in opposite directions, will easily come undone. Although you may lose a collar occasionally, at least you can be sure that your cat should not come to harm when wearing one of this type.

Territories

When your cat goes outside for the first time in a new environment, it will

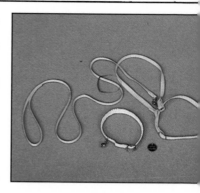

Above: *Be sure to choose an elasticated collar for your cat. A leash may be useful as well.*

inevitably enter the existing territories of other cats in the neighbourhood. This can give rise to conflicts and, when threatened, your cat may either decide to retreat, or stand its ground.

Cats do not depend primarily on vocal communication to convey their reactions, and they have evolved a set sequence of gestures which reveal their intentions to a potential rival. A submissive cat will tend to lie down, as close to the ground as possible, lowering its ears at the same time and tucking its head into its body when threatened.

This is just the first in a series of signals which serve to reduce the risk of actual physical conflict. Subsequently, it may actually roll over on to its back, or seek to escape, in which case there is unlikely to be any contact between the two cats, although the aggressor may chase the fleeing cat for a short distance.

The likelihood of a direct encounter is increased if there is no way that the submissive cat can escape. It will then issue a warning that it intends to defend itself, by hissing and snarling menacingly at the aggressor. As a further deterrent, the cat under threat will stand at its maximum height, arching its back at the same time, and growling loudly. If the aggressor still insists on approaching, effectively trapping the other cat, then a violent encounter becomes inevitable.

In the urban environment, domestic cats do not establish large territories

Above: *Domestic cats still retain the territorial instincts apparent in their wild relatives.*

as a general rule, partly because of their relatively high population densities. In addition, a large territory to provide food is not required, since this is obtained from their owners. Perhaps not surprisingly, feral cats living wild therefore tend to show stronger territorial tendencies than

Below: *Threat gestures are commonly seen, but usually only intact males will fight each other.*

their domestic counterparts.

Female cats generally have more restricted ranges than toms, but will still defend this area against newcomers, until a degree of tolerance is established towards the perceived intruder.

While neutered cats of either sex behave in a similar way to queens, intact toms will certainly prove more aggressive, and more liable to suffer some injuries from fighting. This is because whenever two intact toms meet the prescribed order of dominance will be under threat. Neither views itself as the submissive individual, and unless one backs down, a direct physical confrontation will be inevitable.

The territory of the tom will be clearly marked by means of urine, which is sprayed vertically over objects within its range. Female cats will also spray droplets of urine when in breeding condition, and this may evoke the reaction described as flehmening.

A tom's typical response to this is as if he has come across an unpleasant odour, but in reality, the raising of the neck and curling of the lips causes the scent to pass to Jacobsen's organ,

where the odour is emphasized. The sexual state of the female is directly ascertained, and the tom is likely to seek her out for mating purposes.

Hunting behaviour

Some cats prove more dedicated and effective hunters than others, and to some extent this skill may be inherited. Farmyard kittens often grow up to be highly effective rodent catchers as a result. Yet the hunting behaviour of cats can prove distressing, especially when they catch fledgling birds, or injure fish in a garden pond. It is not possible to eliminate the hunting instinct, but certainly the cat's early life does have an influence on its later desire to catch live prey.

In the wild, up to the age of about six weeks, the kittens see only dead prey which has been caught by their mother. After this stage, she will return with living prey, which the kittens learn to kill. Studies suggest that if they are not exposed to this experience by the age of five months old, then the kittens will not prove very effective hunters in later life.

Many of the games played by the domestic cat in the home reflect the animal's natural hunting instincts. Tossing a toy in the air, leaping on to a piece of rope being pulled along the floor, and pawing at a ball are all aspects of the cat's normal behaviour which have become modified in domestic surroundings.

Below: *The stages in catching prey. Cats are efficient hunters, killing prey with their long canine teeth.*

Hunting cats tend to dispatch prey quite rapidly, and swallow it shortly afterwards. They tend to avoid attacking creatures which they would not be able to eat easily, although this does not always apply, particularly in the case of birds.

In contrast, pet cats are often uncertain of their need to hunt, and are more likely to play with prey, having caught it. Mice are especially favoured for this purpose, being pawed if they fail to respond. In many cases, once the unfortunate creature is actually dead, the cat will not then consume its corpse, although it may continue playing with the body for a time.

This behaviour often seems extremely cruel, but the cat cannot perceive its actions in this sense. It is displaying an instinct which, in its domesticated state, is no longer required, yet the animal's inner need for such action remains strong, and this serves to confuse the cat.

There is unfortunately little that you can do to prevent a cat from hunting, although you can make its task somewhat harder, by fitting a bell to its collar. Neutering has no impact whatsoever on hunting instincts, although it can control other undesirable behavioural traits such as spraying.

Some cats can adapt to the presence of a bell: since they hunt to a great degree by stealth, they may be able to move sufficiently slowly that the bell does not sound until they actually strike at their chosen prey.

It is not recommended to let your cat eat any animals which it catches, since these may present an

CATCHING PREY

1. Approaches prey stealthily

2. Lunges for the prey

Above: *The playful habits of cats are frequently a reflection of their basic hunting instincts.*

unnecessary threat to its health. Many rodents carry immature tapeworms, which in turn will affect any cats which consume them. Other diseases, too, can be transmitted in this way. Parasites passed on by this route include toxoplasma, with its risks to public health (see pages 51 and 88), and lungworm.

Cats, like all carnivores, tend to catch the weaker, often sick animals. For this reason, rodents are particularly hazardous, since the weaker ones could be those affected by warfarin poisoning (rat poison). This anti-coagulant drug will have similar effects on cats, with potentially lethal results.

On occasions, instead of actually consuming the prey itself, the cat will return home with the creature, and offer it to a member of the family. This behaviour is most common in female cats, and is a reflection of their natural instinct to bring back food for their litter. Do not scold your cat under these circumstances therefore: simply show your appreciation and remove the corpse.

You will have to be particularly careful if you have a cat flap, since your cat may then decide to carry its prey into the home itself. This is another reason for fixing the cat flap on a conservatory door, if possible, rather than permitting direct entry to the house via this route.

Cats will also have to be watched carefully with smaller domestic pets, both inside and outside the home. Uncovered fish tanks sited on a convenient table, a bird in a cage or even a guinea pig in an open run on the lawn are all potentially at risk. Take the appropriate measures to protect these pets by placing them out of the cat's reach, and do not leave your cat alone in a room housing a pet bird.

In the garden, take care to site a bird table in a clear position, so that the cat will have difficulty in creeping up and grabbing a feeding bird. Nestboxes should also be positioned carefully, so that the likelihood of the cat reaching the breeding site is reduced. It may be possible to prevent the cat from climbing here by wiring off the base of the tree.

In any event, delicate or newly-planted trees should be protected at their bases from the cat's claws. It can otherwise destroy a young sapling by using it as a scratching post.

Cats and plants

Cats out of doors will often be seen eating grass, typically young shoots, rather than dry stalks. The reason for

3. Catches prey, but does not kill it

4. Plays with the live catch

5. Deals prey fatal bite to the neck

this behaviour is unclear but it may be linked to a need for fibre in the diet. In some cases, often when they have hair-balls, or a heavy burden of intestinal worms, cats deliberately use grass as an emetic (to make themselves vomit).

This should not be confused with regular consumption of grass, which is quite normal, and may help to provide vitamins lacking in meat, typically those of the Vitamin B complex.

In order to ensure that your cat does not eat grass which has been contaminated by chemical residues, you may want to use one of the special container packs enabling you to grow a supply of fresh grass for your cat. This can be very useful for cats living indoors on a permanent basis, and should help to protect houseplants, since these may be eaten instead if no grass is available.

Below: *An example of a typical outside unit of a cattery. The double entrance prevents escape.*

Some popular houseplants are poisonous, and so should be kept away from cats, in case they are tempted to nibble the growing shoots.

In the garden, most cats will be attracted to catnip plants, sometimes also known as catmint *(Nepeta cataria).* It usually appears to produce a sense of well-being when the cat rubs against the plant or occasionally nibbles the leaves. The active chemical which is believed to induce this state has been identified as nepetalactone.

While it has a similar chemistry to various hallucinogenic drugs, at least one-third of cats will not respond to catmint, nor does the plant hold any attraction for young kittens. Once the effects wear off, the cat will then ignore the plant, and not try to repeat its experience immediately.

Outside accommodation
While most people prefer to allow their cats to roam freely, you may decide to construct an outside cattery,

OUTSIDE CATTERY

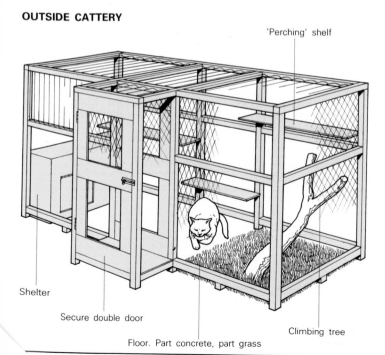

'Perching' shelf

Shelter

Secure double door

Floor. Part concrete, part grass

Climbing tree

Above: *An Abyssinian taking advantage of the space provided by the outdoor attachment to a cattery. Providing areas for exercise is very important.*

particularly if your animals are valuable. A design similar to that of an outdoor aviary will be suitable, composed of an outdoor run linked to a shelter.

You can purchase a cattery of this type from one of the specialist firms which construct animal buildings, and they may be prepared to erect it on site for you. Check in advance that you will not be contravening any planning requirements.

You may prefer to design your own cattery and this should be straightforward, but it will entail building a secure unit. It can be very difficult to catch a cat that escapes from its quarters.

A stout framework composed of 5 cm (2 in) square timber is to be recommended, but if you treat the woodwork, ensure that the preparation used is safe for cats. Many such chemicals are liable to be toxic, including creosote. Stout mesh should be fixed over the individual frames. If you build a sectional structure in the first instance, it will be much easier to expand or move this at a later date as required.

It is best to incorporate a double-doored entry system which should prevent the cats from escaping from the enclosure. Expand the framework therefore around the external door of the run, providing scope for an additional door here. This can then be opened and closed before the cattery itself is entered, thus ensuring the cats within can only escape into the wired area, and not out into the garden.

It will be useful to vary the floor covering in the run. A concrete base can be cleaned off easily and thoroughly, but will prove rather hard for the cat's feet. A small grassed area will therefore be appreciated, but whether or not it is possible to incorporate this effectively will depend to some extent on the location concerned.

A tree trunk enabling the cats to

59

exercise their claws, plus climbing shelves, is a good idea. Some protection against the elements, in the form of translucent plastic sheeting, will also be required on the roof and sides of the run.

In the shelter, you can provide heat, in the form of an infra-red lamp. Choose one of the dull-emitter types, since these act just as a heat source, producing no light. Alternatively, you may prefer to instal a convector heater or a tubular greenhouse heater which operates on the same principle.

In any event, ensure that the cats are not able to reach either the electrical apparatus or the wiring, which they may attempt to chew, with fatal consequences. This is best located in a small corridor behind the pen, with the second entry door in this instance being located within the building rather than outside it.

There is no need to have a separate door connecting the run with the shelter, provided that the cats can move back and forth through a cat flap. Obviously, during the warmer part of the year, the heating may not be required, but you should include a thermostat in the system.

The temperature in the shelter should not be allowed to fall much below 10°C (50°F), with a higher figure often being recommended for sparsely-coated breeds, such as the Devon Rex. Apart from heating, you may also want to have lighting available, so you can check the cats during the winter, after dark.

A year in the life of your cat

The best time to obtain a kitten is just before spring starts, so that your new pet can settle down in its surroundings when the weather is less inclement, and you should be able to spend more time with the cat out of doors.

At this time of the year, the hunting instincts of cats are liable to be honed by the presence of many newly-fledged birds. Try to reduce the likelihood of your cat catching them, but if your attempts fail, you may actually be able to rescue an injured bird. Sadly, even if it appears relatively undamaged, there is a distinct possibility that the bird may already

have received a fatal wound, since a cat bite will inject deadly bacteria from its mouth deep within the tissues of the bird.

Antibiotic cover is therefore essential in such cases, however minor the injury might appear. Your veterinarian should be able to put you in touch with an animal welfare group which caters for sick and injured birds, so that if possible your avian casualty can be expertly rehabilitated.

Holiday time

If you are planning to go on holiday during the summer, you will need to make arrangements for the care of your cat during the period you will be away. Unlike dogs, it is not usually possible to take a pet cat with you on a domestic holiday, simply because of the cat's lifestyle. With a cat that walks on a leash and harness, it might be feasible, but the experience of travelling is liable to prove upsetting

Right: *When moving your cat by car in the summer beware of heat stroke. Never leave it alone.*

Below: *A Turkish Van out for a walk with its owner. Some cats will accept a leash and harness without problems, after early training. But watch out for dogs!*

for your cat and it may run off at the earliest opportunity.

Certainly if you intend to cross national boundaries you must not take any pet, because of regulations to prevent the spread of rabies, without checking the position in advance. Otherwise, you are liable to find yourself being prosecuted and your cat will be either destroyed or placed in quarantine for a period of six months, which is by itself a costly penalty.

Depending partly on how long you intend to be away for, it may be best to find a friend or neighbour who will look after your cat. Over a weekend, this will not be an excessive burden, but remember that a period of several weeks is likely to be a different proposition! The cat should not be moved from its usual environment, unless it can be kept permanently

inside until your return. Ensure that there is an adequate supply of food available: it can be useful if your cat will eat dried food over this period, since this will not turn mouldy and can be fed *ad libitum*.

You must stress to the person looking after your cat that water must be constantly available alongside the dried food.

In spite of their rather solitary natures cats do appreciate human company, and this sort of arrangement for holiday care has obvious shortcomings in this regard. Your friend may not actually see your cat every day, and this can be a source of worry. You will also need to have a cat flap fitted in your door, through which the cat can enter and leave your home, feeding and sleeping inside as it wishes.

Boarding catteries

The other option when you are away is to arrange a place for your cat at a boarding cattery. There are a large number of such establishments, and if possible, obtain a personal recommendation from a friend, or ask your veterinarian for advice. It is well worth arranging an appointment to visit the cattery, prior to making a definite booking. This will enable you to see the facilities available, and also to meet some of the staff.

Obviously, the surroundings are important, and need to be clean. The cats should not be mixed in groups, unless they are used to each other, since this will be unduly stressful, and fighting under these conditions will be almost inevitable at some stage.

During the winter check on the provision of heat, especially if you have a thin-coated Rex cat for example, and the bedding facilities. Talk to the staff - they can provide a good indication of the standard of care at the premises concerned.

Above: *Your cat may be distressed after a journey to the cattery, but sympathetic staff will be on hand.*

Below: *Some cats can be very fastidious about feeding, especially when away from home.*

If you decide to make a reservation, find out what the cattery expects you to provide for your cat. Since cats can be very fastidious about food, especially in unfamiliar surroundings, and may simply refuse to eat if confronted with unfamiliar items, the cattery may request you to bring a supply of your cat's usual food. A favourite piece of bedding, such as an old blanket, will also help the cat to settle in while you are away.

Reputable catteries generally insist that all cats are inoculated. They will want to see evidence that this has been carried out, and that all vaccinations are current. You can usually provide this information in the form of the cat's vaccination certificate, but if you have mislaid this, contact your veterinarian, who will have corresponding records available.

Ask for a letter to confirm that your cat's vaccinations are up-to-date, and this should be accepted by the cattery, although you may have to pay your veterinarian a fee for issuing what is in

Above: *An outdoor attachment to a cattery. This provides more space for exercise. Note the platform provided for the cat to rest on.*

Left: *This blue cream Cornish Rex is settling in to its temporary accommodation. Catteries should always be able to offer heated indoor units.*

effect another certificate. Obviously, if your cat has any particular health problems, explain this to the cattery in advance, especially if regular medication is necessary.

They may not have sufficient staff available to provide nursing care, and you should therefore refer back to your veterinarian for advice. It is possible that the veterinary hospital may look after your cat under these circumstances, particularly if it is for just a short period of time. In any

event, do not forget to provide the cattery with written details about your veterinarian, and preferably a telephone number where you can be contacted in an emergency.

During peak holiday periods, it will probably be impossible to find a vacancy for your cat at most catteries. Try to book as early as possible therefore, immediately you have decided on the dates of your holiday. Satisfied clients will return every year to the cattery of their choice, so you should book quickly.

Seasonal changes
When the weather is hot, especially over a period of time during the summer, your cat may be at risk from the effects of sunburn. While this condition is rare in most of Europe, it can be quite common in Australia and areas within the tropics. The ears are most likely to be affected, particularly

if these are white: indeed, white cats generally are most prone to sunburn.

If you suspect that your cat could be susceptible, try to keep it inside during the warmest part of the day. In addition, use a suitable barrier cream on the ears to protect against the sun's ultra-violet light.

Below: *In spring, the reproductive activity of cats increases again, with toms seeking likely partners.*

The signs of sunburn will initially simply be a reddening of the ears, notably at the tips and around the sides, and possibly a mild degree of irritation. There is a risk that prolonged exposure will lead to the development of skin cancer and surgery, including removal of the affected part of the ear, may then be required.

The cat's coat also changes to reflect the seasons and, with the onset of autumn, the fur may become

Right: *Your cat may require a litter tray if the weather becomes very bad during the winter.*

Left: *As winter approaches cats develop thicker coats which serve to protect them during cold weather.*

thicker, to afford the cat more protection during the colder days of winter. During the following spring the cat will shed these hairs, and this is the major period of moulting, although some hairs will be shed throughout the year. Regular grooming at this time is especially important, in order to prevent the repeated occurrence of hair-balls.

As winter approaches, it is particularly important that your cat is encouraged to come inside at night. You are likely to find, especially with older individuals, that they will in fact spend long periods indoors at this time of year. In bad weather, when the ground is frozen or covered with snow, it may be best to provide your cat with a litter tray indoors. Cats normally bury their faeces in the garden, but this will not be possible until the ground has thawed out.

There is a risk, especially when the temperature remains below zero both

day and night, that your cat could develop symptoms of frostbite. This is not easy to detect in some cases. As the ear flaps tend to be most exposed they will feel very cold, and the cat may fail to react if you gently pinch the skin here.

If you suspect that your cat is affected with frostbite, either on its ears or paws (in which case it will be reluctant to walk) do not try to warm the skin up quickly, as this will prove counter-productive. Immerse the paw in warm water if possible, or alternatively bathe the affected area using cotton-wool. This will restore the circulation gradually, but seek veterinary advice in any event. If the damage is severe, the tip of the ear may ultimately be lost.

Towards the end of the winter, queens start to become sexually active again, as a result of the increase in day length. Toms are more likely to wander from this stage onwards, especially as spring approaches. Do not be surprised if your intact tom disappears for periods of several days at this stage.

Neutering will curb this urge, and should be considered if only for this reason. By the time the breeding period ceases, around the following autumn, an intact tom is likely to be in poor condition and, almost inevitably, will be bearing the scars of battle with other male cats in the area.

BREEDING OR NOT

No owners can afford to ignore the sexuality of their cat, even if they have no intention of using the animal for breeding purposes, since it will have a considerable influence on their pet's behaviour. The age of maturity actually varies somewhat, depending on the breed concerned. Some Siamese may be reproductively active by only 14 weeks of age, although most do not attain puberty until they are about five months old.

Longhairs (Persians) are less precocious, and queens are unlikely to start calling before the age of about ten months. Indeed, if puberty coincides with the onset of winter, it is likely that the first heat will not occur until three or four months later. Tom cats tend to mature slightly later than queens, but they should be sexually competent within 12 months.

The reproductive cycle

The signs of heat in the female cat are usually quite evident. At the start of the cycle, known as the pro-oestrus phase, queens become restless, and overtly affectionate. Subsequently, during the oestrus period when the cat will accept a mate, she will often roll about on the floor, howling, and this noise has given rise to the term of 'calling' as a description for the female's oestrus period.

Although it may appear that she is in pain, this vocalization is quite usual and need not be a cause for concern. Do not be surprised if a queen starts spraying, as this is also normal behaviour at this time, serving to attract tom cats. If you exercise the cat in the garden on a leash, you are likely to find that her urine will bring forth a number of local suitors. For this reason, she should be kept firmly indoors with a litter tray.

The cat is described as an induced ovulator, and in this respect it differs from most mammals, since the ova (eggs) are not shed at a precise time. Instead, ovulation is stimulated by mating, a trait shared with rabbits and ferrets. This ensures that fertilization will almost inevitably occur, as sperm is already present in the reproductive tract prior to the release of the ova. After mating, the cat's behaviour will soon return to normal, but if this does not occur, the signs of oestrus should gradually subside within a fortnight.

There should then be a period of

Below: *The spraying of urine is most commonly associated with toms, but queens show similar behaviour. Pheromones present in their urine serve to attract males.*

dioestrus, before the cycle starts again, about a week later, assuming that the queen is not pregnant. You will need to watch her closely, especially during oestrus, since she will be very keen to escape outside in search of a mate at this stage.

The actual length of the oestrus cycle will vary somewhat, depending partly on age, and on the breed of cat. In some cases, especially Siamese, there may be no dioestrus interval, and queens will call persistently for several months. This can be extremely difficult with a family cat. Yet it will not be possible for you to have the cat neutered if you want to use it later for breeding purposes, and in any case it is not recommended during this period.

The best solution under these circumstances therefore is to stimulate ovulation, and this task can be undertaken by your veterinarian if you wish. It will entail the insertion of a sterile instrument about 1 cm (½ in) into the vagina. Lubricating jelly should be applied to assist the passage of the probe, and usually the cat will be quite vocal throughout the procedure, while the probe is gently rotated in its vagina.

The effect of inducing ovulation follows the pattern of a normal pregnancy, except of course that no kittens result. This phase is described as pseudopregnancy, and subsequently, after about six weeks, the cat's reproductive cycle will be resumed. Persistent calling of this type is sometimes described as nymphomania.

The changes which take place in the queen's cycle are controlled by body substances called hormones. Follicle-stimulating hormone (FSH), released from the part of the brain known as anterior pituitary, stimulates the ovaries to produce the ova (eggs), in fluid-filled containers called follicles. These liberate the hormone oestrogen, which causes the typical behaviour that is associated with the oestrus period.

Below: *This table shows the different stages in the reproductive cycle of a mated queen.*

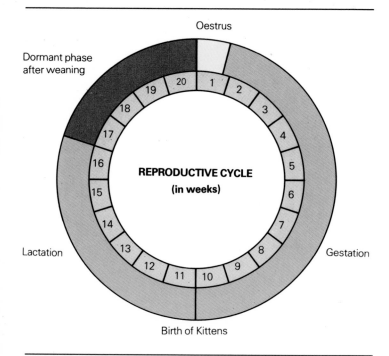

When the ova are liberated from the follicles, they should be fertilized by the sperm travelling up to the uterine horns. It is here that the fertilized eggs or zygotes actually implant, and ultimately, placental connections will develop, nourishing the developing embryos. An average litter comprises between three and six kittens, although variations from these figures are not unknown.

Mating

You must give careful consideration as to what will become of the kittens before you allow your cat to breed. It is much harder to find homes for cross-bred kittens, compared with pedigree offspring. It may well be preferable to have the cat neutered at the earliest opportunity therefore, rather than adding to the already large numbers of unwanted cats and kittens. There is no truth whatsoever in the tale that a queen which has had a litter before neutering will be a more amenable companion in later life.

As it is virtually certain that a queen will soon become pregnant if allowed to roam freely, most breeders go to great lengths to protect pedigree cats from a casual encounter with the neighbourhood tom. This will entail extra work, and can prove somewhat

Above: *Stud houses are used for controlled matings. Stud and queen are separated until mating.*

Right: *The mating process in cats may appear violent, with the tom biting at the back of the queen's neck. However mating can only be initiated by the female lying in the posture described as lordosis.*

harassing in the home, with the queen wanting to go outside at every opportunity during oestrus. Even in an outdoor run however, she will serve as a magnet to male cats in the locality.

It is usual practice not to mate a queen until she has had at least one heat, and, in the case of precocious breeds, not until they are nearly a year old. The actual choice of a stud tom will be influenced by your hopes for the kittens. If you are planning to build up a show line, you should obviously choose another pedigree cat as the sire, and preferably one from a well-known stud.

Study the show results for your particular breed, and approach a fellow breeder and exhibitor who is doing well with his or her cats. Ask if there is a stud tom available, and then arrange a convenient time to visit, so that you can discuss all the necessary matters,

confirmation that she has undergone the FeLV test. Check with the owner of the tom beforehand on these details, so there is no confusion when you actually arrive with your cat.

When first introduced to the male, the queen will be kept in a separate compartment of the pen for a brief period. After the journey, she should soon settle down, and will display the typical signs of oestrus behaviour. It is usual not to handle her at this stage, since some queens become very pugnacious when they detect the scent of the tom.

Once she is displaying, rubbing along the bars and attempting to reach the tom, the two cats can be allowed to mix freely. When she is ready to mate, the queen will raise her rear quarters, adopting the crouching posture frequently described as lordosis. This enables the tom to have access to her vagina while she lies in a relatively horizontal position.

The actual process of mating is quite brief, and at this stage, it is usual for the tom to bite at the scruff of the female's neck. His penis, covered with small spines at the glans (or tip), serves to induce ovulation, and semen is liberated into the female's reproductive tract.

In a few cases, the queen may have another oestrus period after she has already conceived. She will attempt to mate and, if successful, the new zygotes (fertilized eggs) will join those already embedded in the uterine walls. Obviously, the developing kittens will then be of varying ages.

This condition, described as superfoetation, is likely to become apparent about three weeks following the first mating, at the time that the female would normally be entering another cycle. It can affect about one in ten cats. The end result is that the kittens conceived at the first mating are usually born normally, but their younger siblings tend to emerge at the same time, and their chances of survival are very remote.

On rare occasions, the queen may give birth to her two sets of offspring separately, in which case the prognosis may be more favourable for the younger kittens.

and see the stud cat in familiar surroundings. If you are happy that the tom is the type of cat which you are looking for, to complement the characteristics of your own queen, ask about the stud fee.

Costs vary quite widely, depending upon the status of the stud and the bloodline concerned. You could find that the owner of the tom may settle for a share of the resulting kittens, especially if your queen is of good pedigree as well. Check whether another mating will be granted free of charge if the first session fails to provide any offspring.

It is usual practice to move the queen to the tom, rather than vice versa. You will also need to take her vaccination certificate, and possibly

The period of pregnancy

The normal gestation period for the domestic cat is approximately nine weeks, with the litter usually being born in the period from 63 to 66 days following mating. Kittens can survive if born within a week either side of these dates, but beyond this they are unlikely to survive, if indeed they are born alive. There appears to be no real difference between the various breeds in regard to the gestation period, but queens with larger litters tend to give birth relatively early.

At first, it will not be apparent whether or not the mating was successful. It is essential that the queen is kept indoors and away from other toms following her return from the stud. Otherwise, if she is still in oestrus, she may mate yet again with another tom, and a litter containing kittens sired by both males is then likely.

The earliest external sign of a successful mating will become apparent about three weeks later. The nipples of the queen, especially if she has not given birth before, start to swell in size and become noticeably pinker. Breeders sometimes describe this phase as 'pinking up'.

The queen will show no real behavioural changes up to this point, although sometimes vomiting can occur. This of course need not be just a sign of pregnancy, and if you are concerned about your cat's health for any reason, consult your veterinarian.

It is well worth arranging for a check-up in any case, around four and a half weeks after mating, since at this point it should be possible for the veterinarian to feel the foetuses within the horns of the uterus.

Do not attempt this procedure yourself though, as in inexperienced hands the result can be damaging. By this stage, the young kittens will be about 2·5cm (1 in) in length, with the major growth phase of the pregnancy still to follow. It is unfortunately not possible to establish precisely how many kittens your cat is carrying within her uterus at this point. Yet certainly when more than a couple are present, a noticeable swelling of the abdomen is likely to occur from about five weeks onwards.

The kittens grow rapidly in size during the final three weeks of the pregnancy, once their body systems

Below: Queens need a quiet and secluded retreat, such as a box, where they can have their kittens.

Above: *The queen's appetite increases during the last third of pregnancy as the kittens grow.*

have formed. By seven weeks of age, their skeletal outline can be clearly detected on X-ray film, but this procedure is not undertaken routinely since it can be harmful. As the time of birth approaches, their mother will become more restless, seeking out a suitable place where she can give birth. A slight whitish discharge from the vulva at this stage is not unusual.

Caring for a pregnant cat
During the early stages of her pregnancy, your cat can be treated as normal. Do not worry if she still insists on jumping and climbing; this will in fact help to keep her muscles toned up, and can assist with the actual birth process. It is important to take care when handling her, however, so as not to squeeze her abdomen.

Her food intake will increase noticeably only during the final third of the pregnancy, when the kittens are growing to their birth size, weighing in at about 115g (4oz) each. By this point, because of the compression of her stomach, she will not be able to eat large meals, and thus her feeding regimen will need to be modified. Let her eat as much as she appears to want, offering food perhaps four times a day.

At this stage it is especially important that she receives a balanced diet, and even if you usually offer just fresh foods, a complete canned ration is preferable throughout the period of pregnancy, and during the subsequent suckling phase. When you take her to the veterinarian for a check-up, ask for a deworming preparation, since this should help to reduce the level of infection in the kittens when they are born.

Supplements are not usually required when the queen is receiving a balanced diet, but if you are concerned, discuss this with your veterinarian. Excessive use of such preparations throughout the pregnancy is likely to be counter-productive, although the level of calcium assumes greater importance from five weeks onwards. At this time, the skeletal systems of the young kittens will be developing.

It is advisable to make preparations for the birth early, if only to allow the queen to become familiar with the locality where she is expected to have her kittens. A large cardboard box will suffice for the purpose, but cut off one of the sides in order to allow the queen to enter easily. Paper towelling or an old, clean blanket on top of a thick wad of newspapers in the bottom of the box will also be required at first.

Ensure that the room where the queen is to have her kittens is relatively quiet, since if she feels uncomfortable here, she may give birth elsewhere in the house, even adopting an open drawer for the purpose!

In order to encourage her to use the chosen locality, you can carefully place her within the box, ensuring that food and water are available, and leave her alone in the room for periods.

A litter tray is also to be recommended, as you will not want her giving birth outside in the garden.

Watch to see that she does not become constipated as the time for the birth approaches. If necessary, 5 ml of liquid paraffin can be given over her food at every meal to help rectify the situation.

The birth of kittens
When birth is imminent, make the final preparations. Remove bedding from the kittening box, as this might conceal a kitten following birth, and ensure that you can keep the room warm, around 21°C (70°F). Keep a particularly close watch on your cat at this stage, as she may sneak into a bedroom, for example, and have her kittens there.

Immediately prior to giving birth the queen will appear very restless, and may shred the paper in the kittening box. She may attempt to use the litter box, but to no effect, and will lose interest in food. Inspection may reveal signs of milk in the teats.

Although you should not disturb her unnecessarily to check her temperature, a slight fall from the normal figure of 38.5°C (101.5°F) is likely, immediately prior to birth. You may also be able to detect movement through the cat's abdominal wall, revealing the start of the uterine contractions which herald the second phase of labour. This, however, if done at all, should be done very gently.

These periods of straining will become more pronounced, and gentle words of encouragement may help to soothe the cat's fear, especially if she has not given birth previously. Do not actually interfere, however, unless you are certain that there is a problem. Cats are usually adept at producing kittens, and dystocia (difficulty in giving birth, see page 71 for more details) is not commonly encountered.

The contractions will grow in strength, and when the cat lies down on its flank, the birth of the first kitten is likely to be imminent. This can take 30 minutes or so, depending on the presentation of the kitten. The majority are born head first, and this speeds the delivery process. About one third are so-called 'posterior' presentations, with the hindquarters emerging first. Under these circumstances, the queen may need your assistance to expel the kitten from her body.

If the kitten is not born within five minutes of partially emerging from the queen's vulva, you will need to help. Having washed your hands thoroughly, place a clean towel over the kitten and, very gently, attempt to manipulate it out of the vagina. Hold the kitten either side of its body, in the shoulder region if possible, and obviously avoid squeezing the abdomen.

Once free, the kitten will normally be revived by the licking action of its mother. It is usual for the fluid-filled amniotic sac in which the kitten was enclosed to have ruptured during the birth process. Indeed, a sudden rush

of fluid from the female's vulva may be the first sign that a kitten is about to be born. Alternatively, she may break the amniotic sac as it emerges from her vulva.

If this does not happen by the time the kitten is born, tear the sac using your hands. Check that after the fluid has been dissipated none of the tissue is blocking the kitten's face, as this will interfere with its breathing, and wipe the nostrils to remove any fluid. Then, if necessary, rub the kitten quite vigorously on its side with a towel, and also open its mouth several times with your fingers, to stimulate its breathing. If there is no response, hold the kitten carefully with its head pointing downwards, and gently swing it back and forth. It should very soon begin to show some signs of life.

The placental attachment (the cord) will usually be bitten through by the queen soon after the kitten is born. This served to connect the kitten to the

Left: *This queen is clearly pregnant. The major growth phase of the kittens occurs during the last third of the gestation period.*

Below: *Kittens should pass through the birth canal one at a time, although they are likely to be positioned in both uterine horns.*

POSITION OF THE FOETUS

Uterus

Foetus

Placenta

Umbilical cord

Kitten born in fluid sac

Vagina

POSITIONS AT BIRTH

1.

2.

3.

1.

When the kitten appears hindquarters first, this is known as a breach birth. It is the most difficult position.

2.

The best and most common position at birth is the anterior position; the head and feet first.

3.

The kitten is in the posterior position when it appears backwards and feet first. This may cause problems if the queen is weak.

placenta, which sustained it through the pregnancy. If the cat is tired as a result of the effort of giving birth, she may be reluctant to break the placental connection. You can undertake the task, ideally tearing the cord carefully. This will send the blood vessels into spasm, which minimizes bleeding.

Take particular care not to pull the part of the cord attached to the kitten, but hold this portion in one hand, and actually tear it with the other. Excessive pulling on the cord is otherwise liable to result in an umbilical hernia.

It is alternatively possible to cut the cord, but tie it off first, using a sterile thread. Then cut on the placental side of the ligature, using a pair of sterile scissors. The thread will help to prevent blood loss at this stage.

The placenta itself should finally be passed, during the so-called third stage of labour. It is a reddish-brown piece of tissue, and may actually be eaten by the queen soon afterwards. This is an instinctive reaction and is not a sign of impending cannibalism.

Watch closely for the appearance of the placentae: there should be one following each kitten. In some cases, one or more may stay inside the queen, and this will probably need medical treatment later. Unless you have counted them carefully as they came out, you may think you have missed some when in fact the queen has simply eaten them.

Once the first kitten has been born, the remainder usually follow quite quickly, and the whole litter may be produced in rapid succession, within several hours. On rare occasions the queen may cease having contractions, then enter labour again soon afterwards, producing more kittens perhaps a day later.

Watching the birth process can prove to be a worrying time, and if you are concerned at any stage, call your veterinarian for advice. This is particularly important if the cat appears to weaken after contractions have begun, and yet produces no kittens. The first kitten should be born within two hours of the second stage of labour commencing.

If this does not occur, there may be a

Above: *These young cream Burmese kittens are just ten hours old. Avoid disturbance at this stage.*

blockage in the pelvic area which is causing an obstruction. It may result from a previous fracture of the hip, which has healed but created a slight malformity. With a queen that is known to have suffered a pelvic injury of this type, you should consult your veterinarian beforehand, as under these circumstances a Caesarian operation may be inevitable.

Foetal pecularities can interfere with the birth process. In the case of Longhairs (Persians), which usually have relatively small litters, the size of the kittens' heads can cause them to become stuck in the birth canal. Various malpresentations may also occur when the kitten is in the wrong position, and if a kitten becomes badly twisted, this will lead to an obstruction.

Occasionally, two kittens may even become stuck in the uterus at the same time. In rare cases deformity may cause dystocia, when 'monsters' of grotesque appearance are eventually produced.

Your veterinarian will be able to advise you on the best course of action in an individual case. A Caesarian operation may be necessary, and usually this can be carried out quite safely, although the kittens' chances of survival will depend to some extent on how long the birth process has been delayed.

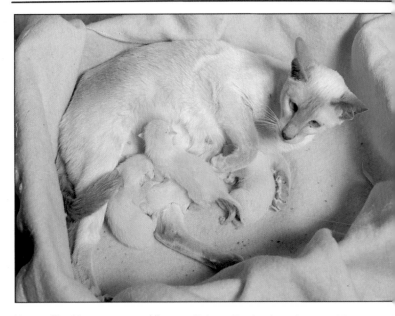

Above: *The kittens start suckling soon after birth, and obtain vital colostrum to protect them against infection during their early life.*

Below: *By the time they are 14 days old, the kittens will have established an order of dominance for the favoured hind teats.*

The post natal period

Under normal circumstances, once her litter is completed the queen will rest, licking her kittens and allowing them to suckle. It is important that they do receive milk from their dam at this stage, because the so-called first milk or colostrum contains the protective antibodies which will help to give the young kittens immunity against disease during the early part of their lives.

For this reason, your veterinarian may have recommended giving the queen a booster inoculation just prior to, or soon after, mating. During pregnancy, only killed (dead) vaccines can be safely administered. These will serve to boost the queen's antibody level, and in turn can assist her kittens.

Do not interfere unduly with the kittens at this stage. Most cats are extremely diligent, and are very protective towards their offspring. If, however, you suspect that there could be a kitten with a congenital defect, such as a cleft palate, you should remove this from the litter.

The obvious external sign of this condition is milk running out of the nostrils, as a result of an improper covering to the roof of the mouth. Take the kitten to your veterinarian: treatment is not usually practical, and affected individuals are painlessly euthanased.

Ensure that the queen has a readily available source of fluid, constantly replenished. When suckling her litter, she will drink an increasing volume, in order to compensate for the loss of fluid in her milk. You can offer milk regularly, as well as water, but if your

Above: *All kittens have blue eyes at first, with the change to adult coloration occurring once they are about three months old.*

cat is allergic to cow's milk, you may want to try one of the special milk substitutes which are used for hand-rearing kittens. These are formulated specifically for cats, and thus adverse reactions are far less likely to arise than with cow's milk.

The feeding regimen should continue as during the latter part of pregnancy, with four meals being provided daily. It is best to feed to satisfy the queen's appetite. Her food consumption may vary somewhat, depending on the number of kittens in the litter.

At first, the young kittens will suckle every couple of hours or so, and are relatively quiet. Persistent restlessness and crying at any stage is a sign that all is not going well, and it may be that there is insufficient milk for the litter.

Check the queen's nipples carefully for signs of milk. If you discover a teat which appears red and inflamed, as well as being painful, this is probably indicative of a local infection, frequently described as mastitis.

Antibiotic treatment will be required, and you will have to protect the affected teat against the attentions of the kittens until it has recovered.

An order of dominance soon develops within the litter, and those kittens which monopolize the hind teats are liable to grow at a slightly faster rate, since the milk supply here is better. About this time, the queen will start to leave her offspring for short periods.

It is usual for there to be a reddish discharge from the vagina for a period after the birth has taken place, but if you are concerned, contact your veterinarian. This is particularly important if she appears to lose her appetite, and starts to neglect the kittens at this early stage.

Under normal circumstances, the young cats will put on weight at a rate of about 85 g (3 oz) or so per week. By the age of seven days, their eyes will be starting to open, and occasionally you may have to bathe them gently if they become sealed up again. Throughout this period, the queen will groom her kittens, licking them repeatedly, which also serves to encourage them to urinate and defecate. They will become increasingly active as they get bigger.

77

Milk fever and hand rearing

Queens with a large litter are particularly at risk from the condition known as milk fever or eclampsia, once the kittens are over a fortnight old. It results from a shortage of calcium, and the symptoms can be alarming. At first, the cat starts to stagger, and this is rapidly followed by convulsions. Milk fever can be reversed equally quickly, but rapid veterinary assistance will have to be sought, since this is a life-threatening condition.

Subsequently, you may have to reduce the litter size, by fostering some of the kittens to another queen with kittens of a similar age, or hand-rearing them.

This latter task should not be undertaken lightly, since it is a time-consuming task. Once the kittens are over a week old, however, hand-rearing is more straightforward, since they will have received the protective colostrum from their mother. You can obtain special feeders, as well as the milk powder mentioned previously, to assist with this task.

Mix the food for the kittens fresh on each occasion as far as possible. Any that is left over must be stored in a refrigerator until the next feed, and then will need to be warmed up. It should subsequently be discarded, and the feeding vessel must be washed out thoroughly between feeds, using a detergent, before being rinsed thoroughly.

At first, young kittens need to be fed every two hours or so, but by the age of a fortnight, feeds at four-hourly intervals should be adequate. Wipe their faces and bodies with a damp cloth, to mimic the licking action of their mother, and this will encourage defaecation. It is important to keep their surroundings as clean as possible.

Do not force young kittens to take a large quantity of milk. Their appetite naturally tends to be rather limited, and the risk of inhalation pneumonia, caused by the ingestion of fluid into the lungs, is increased if you attempt to rush the feeding sessions. Solid food can be introduced to the diet by the time that the kittens are around

three weeks old, and the temperature of their box can be gradually lowered.

You can obtain special heating pads to provide heat from beneath for young kittens, but make certain that they can move easily to another part of their box if they get too hot. This also applies in the case of hot-water bottles, which should be wrapped adequately, or filled just with tepid water, to ensure that the kittens will not burn themselves.

Weaning

Although kittens may start to sample solid foods around three weeks of age, weaning does not really begin until they are about a month old. At first, they may not be very keen to eat solids, but start by smearing meat on your fingers. The kittens will probably start to sniff this, and may lick at it.

Subsequently, you can place a larger quantity on a saucer, and hold this at a convenient angle for the kittens, having attracted their attention. Start with a little boiled fish, or one of the complete kitten foods which will form the basis of the young cats' diet during the post-weaning phase. They will be less enthusiastic about sampling food from a bowl at this stage.

You will need to supervise feeding sessions, because otherwise the queen is liable to take the food

Above: *The kittens will soon be accepted into the established group of adult cats.*

Below: *Bottle-feeding a kitten. The use of a special feeder and a milk substitute is to be recommended.*

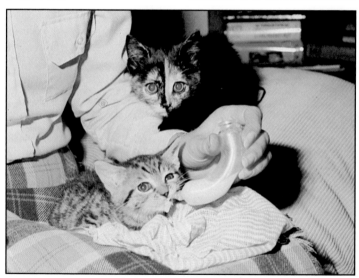

intended for the kittens. Within a week or so, they will be eating quite readily on their own, and by this time will be consuming several ounces of food spread across four meals during the course of the day.

Milk should also be available to the kittens throughout the weaning period, or better still, a milk replacer, made up with water as directed. This will prevent cases of diarrhoea resulting from intolerance of cow's milk occurring.

You should find that the kittens are virtually independent by about two months of age, although in some cases, notably Longhairs, this period may be slightly longer. Pedigree cats

79

must be registered with the appropriate breed authority. In the United States, and other countries where there is more than one registration authority, you may want to register the kittens with several different bodies, especially if you want to show them at a later date. You will be able to enter your cats in a wider range of events as a result.

Control of the breeding cycle
The most effective means of controlling the female's breeding cycle is by the operation known as spaying, but chemical control can be useful if you want to breed from your cat, and are seeking to defer the oestrus period. This should be discussed with your veterinarian, who will be able to advise you on the options available, since there can be side-effects from this, certainly over a period of time.

Generally, long-acting progestogen injections are to be favoured, and these can be administered by your veterinarian. At present, there is no reliable method of controlling fertility in the case of the tom by using chemical means.

Spaying entails the removal of both the ovaries and the uterus. It is usually best carried out when the cat is approaching puberty, certainly by six months of age. If your cat is mature and showing signs of oestrus, your veterinarian will probably recommend waiting until the subsequent period of dioestrus. This is because the hormone oestrogen will increase the blood supply to the uterus, so that the blood loss will be potentially more pronounced if surgery is carried out at this stage.

Spaying is usually a very safe operation, but there is always a slight risk when an anaesthetic is administered. Your veterinarian may ask you to sign a consent form for the operation: this is usual practice, and should not be viewed as a cause for concern.

The incision is usually made on the flank, after the fur has been shaved off over a small area. This will regrow in time, but it may, especially in the case of Siamese, be slightly lighter in

Above: *Neutering a queen will prevent unwanted kittens. The clipped fur soon regrows.*

colour. If you are worried by this, ask your veterinarian about carrying out the surgery via the midline. The incision in this instance is on the lower side of the body in the abdominal region, and obviously will be less conspicuous here.

In fact, the approach does tend to vary on a geographical basis, with the midline incision being more common in the United States than Europe. The only contra indication to midline spaying may be in the case of a very obese cat, since the stitches could rupture more easily in this position, delaying the healing process.

Although your veterinarian may wish to hospitalize the cat overnight, she will have recovered from the anaesthetic by the next day. If, however, she is still under the influence of the anaesthetic when you collect her, keep her in a quiet environment. When coming round, a cat will tend to be disturbed by noise.

There is really no need to restrict your cat's domain to any great extent in the immediate post-operative period, but it is probably best to keep her inside for a few days. This should help to prevent her from leaping around excessively, and pulling out the sutures from the wound. Healing is usually rapid, and the stitches can be removed about a week or so after the operation.

If the stitches do become displaced, you will have to take the cat back to the veterinarian, especially if any tissue protrudes through the incision. It is very difficult to prevent a cat from scratching or biting at the sutures, but in the majority of cases they will not interfere with them.

If you have children, explain to them that the cat is recuperating, and should be left alone, so that they do not inadvertently damage the stitches.

Neutering of the male cat, described as castration, is a more straightforward procedure, again carried out under anaesthetic.

Some owners prefer to wait for slightly longer before having this surgery carried out, simply because the male sex hormone, testosterone, creates the typical broad-faced appearance of the tom cat. Removal of the testicles before puberty will prevent these characteristic changes occurring. However, if the operation is postponed to this later stage, the tom may still continue spraying, although the pungent odour of the urine will be lost following neutering.

It is usual to neuter adult tom cats during the period of sexual quiescence, in late autumn and early winter, but this need not apply in every case. There is a slight risk that removal of the testicles, and thus testosterone, may lead to hair loss at a later date. Replacement hormonal therapy should correct this problem, known as hormonal alopecia, quite satisfactorily.

After neutering, cats of both sexes may show a greater tendency to become obese, and some dietary modifications may be required. Overall though, neutering should ensure that your cat leads a less stressful existence, and has a correspondingly longer life expectancy. It also makes the cat more acceptable within the domestic environment, by overcoming the typical traits associated with feline sexual behaviour.

Below: *Castration of a tom cat entails removal of the testicles and part of each spermatic cord. Spaying a queen involves removal of both the uterus and ovaries.*

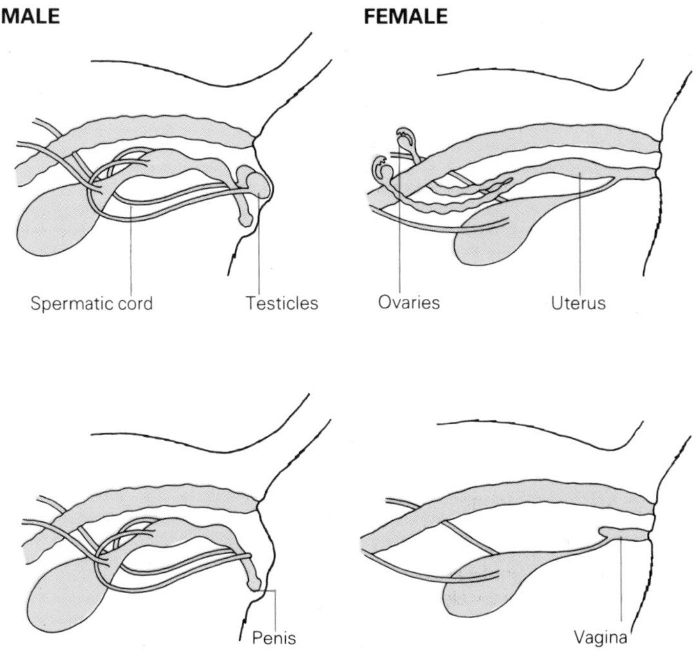

MALE

Spermatic cord   Testicles

FEMALE

Ovaries   Uterus

Penis

Vagina

Having chosen your veterinarian, it can be useful to obtain veterinary insurance for your cat. Depending on the exclusions attached to individual policies, this should mean that you will be covered for veterinary fees above a certain figure, although routine costs such as neutering are excluded, as a general rule.

Insurance can provide considerable peace of mind, especially against the potentially high costs of orthopaedic surgery, if your cat is unfortunately injured in a traffic accident.

It needs to be borne in mind that certain feline diseases, known as zoonoses, can be spread from cats to humans. Undoubtedly the most notorious of these is rabies virus, but a number of parasites can also be transmitted to humans. Injuries resulting from careless handling of cats can also sometimes create considerable problems.

Cat bites will frequently turn septic unless they are carefully cleaned. This applies especially to wounds caused by the canine teeth, which cause deep, puncture-type injuries where tetanus bacteria may thrive.

As a precaution, therefore, seek medical advice when any member of your family is badly bitten if they have not recently had an inoculation against tetanus. In all cases, bathe the wound with a suitable disinfectant, and apply an antiseptic cream.

One quite rare disease of humans, which is linked to cats, is known as Japanese Cat Scratch Fever (Cat Scratch Disease). It was thought that this illness, resulting in a generalized, severe debility and inflammation of lymph nodes throughout the body, was caused by a virus. Recent research, published in the medical journal *The Lancet* during 1985, suggests however that the causal agent is actually a bacterium. possibly *Rothia,* and therefore may respond to antibiotic treatment.

Careful supervision of children with cats is obviously to be recommended, not only from the zoonotic angle. Never leave a young baby alone in a room with a cat, as it may inadvertently smother the child, causing brain damage or even death as a result. The

Above: *A veterinarian carrying out an eye examination, using a ophthalmoscope for the purpose.*

cat will be attracted by the child's body warmth, and will seek to snuggle up alongside the infant.

External parasites
Cat fleas: These are the most commonly encountered external parasites, or ectoparasites as they are sometimes known. Cat fleas will in fact feed on people, if they find themselves displaced from their normal host, but will not be able to breed there. Some cat owners become sensitized to flea bites, rather like cats, and just a single bite can develop into a painful and highly irritating skin swelling.

The flea population reaches a peak during the warmer months of the year. Cats living out of doors for part of the time can acquire fleas from a wide variety of sources, including dogs and even rabbits. In the latter case, the fleas will tend to remain localized around the head, but normally they will be distributed over the whole body.

Although warmth is important in controlling the life cycle of the flea, the relative humidity of the environment is also highly significant. This is a measure of the moisture content of the air. If this is below 50 per cent, then the fleas will not be able to complete their life cycle.

As with other parasites, it is important to have some insight into the life cycle of a flea in order to control

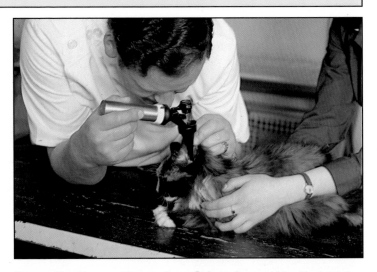

Above: *Checking a cat's ears for infection or ear mites. Treatment can then be given.*

Below: *A general health check is often carried out at the time of the the annual 'booster' inoculation.*

its spread. The eggs are distributed from the cat's body on to bedding, and other sites around the house where the cat sleeps.

Since each female flea can produce 800 eggs, a population explosion will soon take place under favourable conditions, unless their numbers are controlled. It will not be sufficient merely to treat your cat: its environment must also be treated, so as to prevent reinfection.

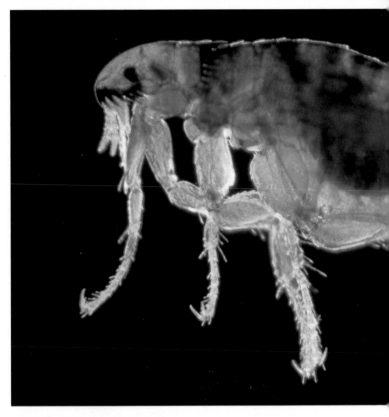

How to combat fleas: If possible, always groom your cat outside, so that if any fleas are present, they should be displaced here, rather than in the home, where they are more likely to bite you or the cat. One of the earliest signs of a flea infestation is likely to be persistent scratching by your cat, and then, on close inspection, you will find the typical flea dirt in the coat.

It is useful to have a container of water available when you groom your cat, so that any fleas which are caught can be easily transferred here, and then disposed of down a drain or toilet. Alternatively, you can kill them by pinching their body, blocking the respiratory pore in the process.

In order to deal with fleas on your cat, you can wash the animal with either an insecticidal shampoo or soap. The former is easier to use, producing a lather. It is not easy to bathe a cat, however, since the majority intensely dislike being immersed in water.

If you do use a wash of any kind to remove your cat's fleas, be certain to read the instructions carefully beforehand. Some products are liable to be toxic for your cat, and will have to be rinsed out of the coat after a prescribed period of time. A large measuring jug is useful for this purpose, but it will be difficult to persuade the cat to remain stationary for this period, certainly out of doors.

You may also be able to use these solutions to wash the cat's bed. One of the best ways to remove the fleas' eggs from the environment, however, is simply to vacuum the area, paying particular attention around edges of carpets, although flea powder may also be useful here.

Powders, sprays and collars: It is often easier to use a powder to control fleas on your cat, but again, watch

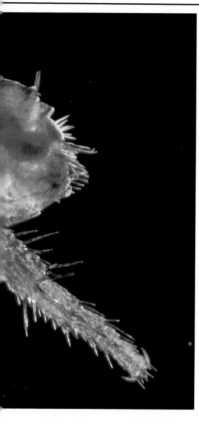

Above: *A cat wearing a plastic Elizabethan collar, which prevents it scratching or biting itself.*

Left: *A cat flea seen under the microscope. These parasites can cause considerable discomfort.*

these chemicals can prove toxic to young cats. Check this carefully on the labelling. Some dog flea treatments are also inappropriate for cats.

Ill effects of the fleas: If the cat does become sensitive to fleas, it will show the symptoms of miliary eczema (itching eruptions of the skin) because of the intensity of the underlying irritation. Scabs form where the cat regularly scratches at the flea bites, and apart from resulting hair loss, these wounds may become infected. Rigorous treatment against fleas will be required, and desensitization, as well as antibiotics to control any infection, may be recommended by your veterinarian. Disinfectants are ineffective against both fleas and their eggs, and should not be used in such cases. Indeed, great care must be taken with disinfectants, since some are toxic for cats.

While fleas act as an intermediate host in the life cycle of the tapeworm *Dipylidium caninum,* they can also transmit blood-borne infections as well. These include the protozoal disease known as feline infectious anaemia. In this case, the micro-organisms attack the red blood cells, causing anaemia and general debility. Diagnosis entails the examination of a blood sample, and treatment, which may include transfusions of blood, often proves successful, certainly in milder cases.

closely for any signs of an adverse reaction, such as excessive salivating. The powder, too, may need to be brushed out of the hair.

The noise of an aerosol spray may upset the cat, and such treatments tend to be relatively costly, compared with powders.

Flea collars are not really safe for cats unless they are elasticated, ensuring that the cat cannot get caught up by the collar. It may be preferable to use a medallion, which simply clips on to an existing elasticated collar, releasing its chemical ingredients over a period of time, although there is some doubt over the efficacy of medallions. Collars must be fitted quite tightly, and may cause an allergic reaction around the neck.

The treatment of young kittens with anti-flea preparations needs to be carried out very cautiously, because

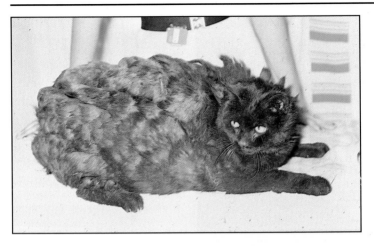

Above: *Mange may result in irritation and skin crusting. It is caused by two types of mite.*

Ticks: Several other external parasites of cats can also transmit diseases when they feed on the cat's blood, and ticks represent a particular hazard. These are more common in rural areas, and attach to the cat's skin, especially around the head, as it moves through vegetation.

Treatment is very simple, but do not resort to pulling the tick out of the cat's skin, because almost inevitably, you will leave the head section embedded, and this can set up a local reaction. Instead, cover the tick with petroleum jelly, and leave it alone. With its respiratory system blocked by the jelly, the tick will fall off intact within a day or so.

Ticks which have not fed are relatively small, but they can swell noticeably in size, and may appear to be a small lump on the cat's skin. If you are uncertain about the cause of the swelling you should ask your veterinarian.

Cats are generally not afflicted with many ticks at once, but occasionally you may discover several. Like fleas, they can cause anaemia when present in numbers, especially in the case of a kitten. Ticks are relatively common in tropical areas, and must be dealt with regularly.

Mites and mange: Other ectoparasites are likely to be far less evident. This applies especially to the mite *Cheyletiella,* the appearance of which is reminiscent of dandruff in the coat, although these mites will move when disturbed. They appear to cause relatively little harm to the cat, living essentially on the surface of the skin, but, in the case of humans, *Cheyletiella* causes an irritating dermatitis (inflammation of the skin).

Mange is generally rare in cats, although when it does occur its effects are clearly noticeable. Typical signs include repeated scratching of the affected area by the cat, thickening of the skin, and scab formation, with some degree of hair loss as well. Mange is usually localized around the head, although it can spread to the paws, as the cat repeatedly attempts to ease the underlying irritation by scratching.

In order to diagnose mange with certainty, your veterinarian may have to take a skin scraping of the affected area, and then examine this under a microscope for signs of the parasites. Treatment is similar to that recommended for fleas, although in this instance tablets may be a more effective cure.

Take particular care to avoid using the grooming tools on other cats, as these can serve to transmit the parasites. Bedding also represents a hazard, and affected cats should be kept on their own until the medication has proved successful.

Both lice and mites are reasonably

easy to treat, since they do not actually live in the cat's environment for any length of time. One exception is the so called Harvest Mite or Chigger which, as its name suggests, is more common in the autumn. The Larval stage of this pest is parasitic, usually attaching on to the cat's paws. These parasites cause intense irritation, but drop off in time to complete their life cycle. Close examination of the paws of an infected cat will reveal the tiny orange-red specks, and treatment such as a flea spray will usually resolve the situation.

Ear mites are often much harder to eliminate successfully, and repeated treatment may be required in this instance. Your cat could acquire these parasites from a dog sharing its home. The mites cause a variable degree of irritation in the ear canal, and the most reliable sign of their presence is when the cat scratches repeatedly at this part of its body. A significant accumulation of wax may be apparent on closer examination.

Using an auroscope, your veterinarian will actually be able to see the mites within the ear, and will provide you with suitable treatment.

Always complete the course as directed, since if you stop early the mites will almost certainly not be eliminated totally, and a recurrence of the symptoms is then likely. Ear infections of this type are often mixed in character, and thus most treatments contain an antibiotic to counter any bacterial involvement, and a steroidal compound to soothe the inflammation.

If the cat repeatedly scratches at its ear it is likely to cause local injury giving rise to a swelling described as a haematoma. The blood vessels will have been ruptured as a result of the constant trauma, causing haemorrhage into the surrounding tissues. A similar injury may result in tom cats which have been fighting, with the ear flap becoming very swollen. Although this may resolve itself to some extent, you should consult your veterinarian for advice in the first instance.

You should obtain treatment as

Below: *A range of the external parasites which can affect cats. A veterinarian is best placed to advise on the correct treatment.*

EXTERNAL CAT PARASITES

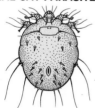

Head mange mite
(Notoedres cati)

Mite *(Trombicula sp.)*

Ear mite
(Otodectes cynotis)

Cat louse
(Felicola subrostratus)

soon as possible if you suspect that your cat has an ear infection. If left, it may spread into the middle ear, causing circling and other behavioural abnormalities. The chances of a full recovery under these circumstances are relatively poor.

Fly strike: Several types of fly can also parasitize cats, and in warm weather especially, you should watch for any soiling of your cat's coat with faecal matter. This will serve to attract blowflies, and they are likely to lay their eggs in the soiled coat. When the maggots hatch, they will burrow away from the light, going beneath the fur and into the cat's tissues.

Known as 'fly strike', this condition is more prevalent in older, longhaired cats, and can actually prove fatal. The maggots produce toxins, and when these enter the circulatory system, they are likely to have far-reaching effects, apart from the local tissue damage caused directly by the parasites.

Treatment entails cleaning the wound, removing all the maggots with tweezers, and counteracting the symptoms of the toxin. Wounds of any kind are another favourite site to which flies will be attracted, and a close watch should be kept on your cat

Below: *Cat faeces are often buried in the garden and may be a health hazard, especially to pregnant women, because of toxoplasmosis.*

if you think it could be at risk.

In parts of the United States, the larvae of *Cuterebra* flies may infect cats, attaching to the skin and boring into the tissues beneath, where they conceal themselves. Kittens are most at risk, and treatment will entail surgical removal of the parasite.

Internal parasites
Protozoans: When the parasite in question is a microscopic animal that has a body consisting of a single cell, this is called a protozoal infection. The most significant of the protozoal diseases of cats is toxoplasmosis (see also page 51), because of the risk which this poses for pregnant women.

Sources of this infection for cats are usually either rodents or raw meat, but clinical signs of the disease are not very noticeable. Yet toxoplasmosis is widespread: over one-third of cats have antibodies to the infection, confirming that at some point in their lives they have been exposed to it.

Once infected, the cat starts to pass oocysts (tiny packets containing the 'eggs' of the parasite) in its faeces about five days later, and continues to do so for as long as three weeks, shedding literally millions of these oocysts during this period. They are not immediately infective on leaving the cat's body, but take several days to mature in the environment. Contained cat litter is liable to be a potent source

of infection, especially if it is not disposed of carefully, preferably in a sealed plastic bag.

Since many cats defaecate out of doors, in a garden, soil can also be hazardous. For these reasons it is advisable for pregnant women to wear gloves when emptying cat litter trays or gardening. It is possible to destroy oocysts with boiling water, so potentially contaminated surfaces should be washed down accordingly.

Persistent diarrhoea can in some cases be traced to another protozoal infection: the disease is described as coccidosis. To confirm this disease, the veterinarian needs to examine a faecal sample, and appropriate treatment can then be instituted.

Kittens are most at risk if they have been kept in dirty surroundings, and the diarrhoea may be bloodstained, as a result of damage to the lining of the intestinal tract. Under these circumstances, the damage may not be fully repaired, so the kitten's growth will be stunted.

Fluid therapy is often necessary to correct the dehydration resulting from the diarrhoea.

Worm infections: A wide variety of parasitic worms can afflict cats: roundworms are most common in kittens, for the reasons described on page 43. Routine deworming will overcome them, and tapeworms also present in the gut. Yet worms may also localize in other parts of the body.

Lungworm is not unusual in hunting cats. They obtain the infection from eating an invertebrate host, such as a snail, or even a bird which has consumed an infective invertebrate. Clinical signs vary, but a persistent cough, especially in a young cat, is a fairly common sign. Once diagnosed, appropriate treatment can be given by your veterinarian.

Heartworms, spread by biting insects, affect cats in tropical areas. Routine preventive measures are recommended, for it is very difficult to kill the parasite once it is inside the heart without obstructing the circulatory system as a result.

Raw fish can spread another group of parasites, known as trematodes or flukes. These tend to localize in the

Internal Cat Parasites

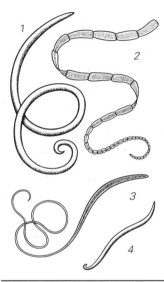

Above: *The principal internal parasites that can affect cats. The drawings show the basic shapes of the parasites and are not in scale with each other. The most common species are listed.*
1 Roundworm (Toxocara canis *and* Toxascaris leonina)
2 Tapeworm (Dipylidium caninum)
3 Whipworm (Trichuris sp.)
4 Hookworm (Ancylostoma caninum)

liver, and are likely to result in jaundice, because they block the flow of bile through the ducts here. In this case, treatment can again be difficult, and so cats should be prevented from eating raw fish as far as possible. Fluke infections are relatively common in parts of North America, but tend to be restricted to certain areas.

Infectious illnesses
Although vaccination has meant that the majority of viral diseases of cats are now far less common, their effects can still be equally devastating when outbreaks do occur.
Feline infectious enteritis (FIE) has a very high mortality associated with it. Between four and ten days after

exposure to the virus, susceptible cats will develop a high temperature, and rapidly fall sick.

Diarrhoea is a persistent feature of the disease and dehydration soon follows, although the cat will drink quite heavily at this stage. A characteristic change in the pattern of the white blood cells has given rise to the other name for this disease, which is feline panleucopaenia. The circulating leucocytes (white blood cells) decline rapidly in number, which will be clear if your veterinarian takes a series of blood samples.

Since FIE is a viral disease, antibiotics are of no real value in combating its effects but fluid therapy may help to sustain the cat. Young individuals are most at risk, and even if they survive, they will probably never recover fully. The damage to the lining of the intestinal tract will be permanent and diarrhoea may then occur at intervals.

If a pregnant queen is infected in the later stages of the gestation period, the virus will cross the placental barrier, and damage the nervous system of her developing kittens. The resulting lack of co-ordination will mean that the kittens, afflicted with cerebellar ataxia, will have to be destroyed at birth. The virus will survive well in the cat's surroundings for over a month, so that thorough disinfection will be necessary following an outbreak of FIE.

FCV and FVR: Respiratory diseases of cats are often of viral origin, although other infectious agents can also be involved. Two separate diseases are of particular significance, with vaccines being available to protect against their effects. Together, they are often described as cat 'flu: feline calicivirus (FCV), which tends to be milder, and feline rhinotracheitis (FVR), which is more vicious in its effects.

Typical symptoms in the case of FCV include ulceration of the tongue, so that the cat is reluctant to eat, in addition to having runny eyes and nose. Although neither virus will survive for long in the environment, they can be spread rapidly in a cattery by airborne droplets, especially when an affected cat is sneezing.

Once infected, cats remain carriers of these viruses for a long time, and represent a threat to others which have not been inoculated. In some cases, after apparently recovering, some individuals relapse, and clinical signs persist, with infection of the sinuses being common.

The mortality rate is variable, tending to be higher in kittens and older cats, where pneumonia is frequently the cause of death. Again, only fluid therapy is of direct value as treatment, but antibiotics may help to prevent serious complications, such as pneumonia or subsequent bacterial infection of the sinuses. Strong-smelling foods, such as sardines in tomato sauce, may encourage a cat to start eating after a bout of respiratory disease. Bathe the nostrils, as any interference with the sense of smell will limit the cat's appetite still further.

Feline leukaemia virus (FeLV): Research into this illness has been stimulated by the human killer disease AIDS, because there are certain similarities between the symptoms of both diseases. There is no evidence whatsoever to suggest that FeLV can be transmitted to humans however, and it is certainly not the cause of AIDS.

After infection with FeLV, (which, if it takes place during pregnancy, causes abortion), some cats will develop antibodies and overcome the disease. If this does not occur, the cats may then develop clinical signs of the disease, which damages the immune system. The effects can be quite varied. Apart from leukaemia, which affects part of the white blood cell population, the bone marrow is also attacked in some instances. As a result, anaemia is commonly associated with FeLV infections.

Since the cat's overall immunity is weakened, it is likely to succumb to a range of diseases, and additionally, tumours may develop in the lymph nodes. The thymus is frequently affected in young cats, and difficulty in breathing may become apparent in this instance, because of the pressure of the trachea in the region of the neck, swallowing may also be similarly

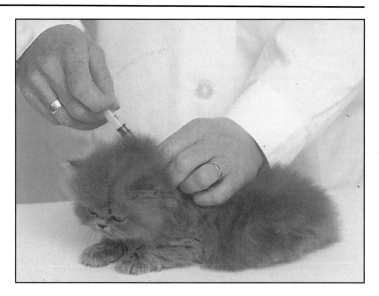

handicapped.

The actual onset of clinical symptoms following infection can vary quite widely, but there is no treatment for FeLV, and confirmed cases should be euthanased, because they represent a persistent threat to the health of others.

In order to ascertain whether the cat is actually suffering from FeLV, rather than just infected, blood tests will be required. These are repeated at an interval of about three months, so that if the first test is positive, the cat will need to be kept in isolation. On the second occasion, the result should prove negative if the cat has produced antibodies to the virus or was already immune. If this is positive, then it is likely that the cat has become a carrier, and clinical signs may then develop in due course.

Conversely, an initial test may be negative, and can then be followed by a positive result. This shows that the virus was probably incubating at the time of the first test, and subsequent testing will be necessary. Once a case is confirmed, the majority of cats affected will be dead within two years. A vaccine offers the best hope of controlling the spread of FeLV, and already, early results from the United States are quite encouraging.

Feline infectious peritonitis: This is

Above: *Inoculations offer vital protection to all cats and cause very little discomfort, as shown.*

another viral disease; it is less common than FeLV, but is invariably fatal. Relatively little is known about this ailment, although it does appear more common in cats living in groups. Young cats, typically under three years of age, are most commonly affected, and early signs of the disease tend to be vague.

The traditional form is characterized by swelling of the abdomen, with an accumulation of fluid here. The membrane lining this part of the body, known as the peritoneum, becomes inflamed. The volume of fluid in the abdominal cavity interferes with the body functions, and may extend into the chest, causing the cat to have difficulty in breathing.

In some cases, there can be a form of FIP infection where no fluid builds up, and this will obviously be less apparent. A common sign is a change in colour of the cat's eyes. Often, an underlying case of FeLV will be detected, once FIP is diagnosed, and it seems likely that FeLV lowers the body's resistance to this other infection. Euthanasia is again the only option, since there is unfortunately no treatment available.

Rabies: This, too, is a virus infection. It is of major significance since it is transmissable to humans. There is no fear of water in cats affected by rabies. The usual route of spread is via a bite, but infected saliva can be equally lethal, if it gains access to the body through a cut. The virus spreads slowly through the nervous tissue, and the incubation period can be prolonged, as long as four months or so in some cases.

The earliest indication of rabies is likely to be a distinct change in the personality of your cat. It may become very nervous, and photophobic (avoiding light). Clear signs will be apparent during the clinical stage of excitement, sometimes described as the 'furious' period.

Although the cat may hide at this time, it will launch into a vicious attack if provoked or disturbed in any way. A quiescent phase, during which the cat becomes paralysed, then follows, being terminated by death.

If you suspect that your cat could be suffering from rabies, seek advice from your veterinarian without delay. Close the animal in a room and make no attempt to touch or approach it. If you are bitten, wash the wound out under a running tap, and get medical help immediately.

In countries where rabies is present in the animal population, you should seek to have your cat inoculated against this disease from the outset. Only by this means can you afford your family protection. In some countries where vaccination is voluntary a significant number of cats are not protected, even though every animal is potentially at risk from this deadly disease.

Key-Gaskell syndrome: now often described as **feline dysautonomia,** this was first diagnosed during 1982 at the Bristol Veterinary School. The actual cause of the disorder has yet to be elucidated, although the clinical signs are now quite clearly identified. The most striking is often the dilation of the pupils of the eyes, which are not affected by light exposure as normal.

This is just one of the manifestations of a breakdown in the functioning of the autonomic nervous system. The third eyelid protrudes across the eyes, reflecting a loss of condition, while other more specific signs include alterations to body functions, causing severe constipation and possibly weakness of the hind limbs.

Body secretions dehydrate, causing the nose to take on a dried appearance. There is little that can be done in the way of treatment, but supportive therapy may help in some cases. The likelihood of a full recovery is not great, however, and euthanasia may ultimately be necessary.

Skin ailments
Ringworm is not a parasitic disease, in spite of its name, but results from a fungal infection. This localizes on the coat, and can create bald patches, although the effects generally tend to be less noticeable. It is a zoonosis, and will cause characteristic red circular lesions in people, typically on the forearms, where the cat is held.

Your veterinarian may be able to confirm ringworm by examining the cat's fur under a special Wood's lamp, but otherwise, skin scrapings and culturing could be necessary. Treatment is generally straightforward, although it can be dangerous for pregnant cats, since the drug used may lead to foetal malformation. Dispose of all grooming tools, and clean the cat's environment thoroughly with a disinfectant as recommended by your veterinarian to eliminate surviving fungal spores. These spores can remain viable for a long period.

Rodent ulcers, in spite of their name, can also affect cats which do not hunt. The cause of the active erosion of tissue around the mouth, normally on the upper lip, is not clear, but it can be treated successfully by various means, including cryosurgery. This freezes the affected tissue, and in time normal healing can be anticipated.

Another localized skin problem sometimes seen is stud tail, normally confined to intact males. This results from the secretions of glands at the base of the tail, which lead to an accumulation of greasy staining here.

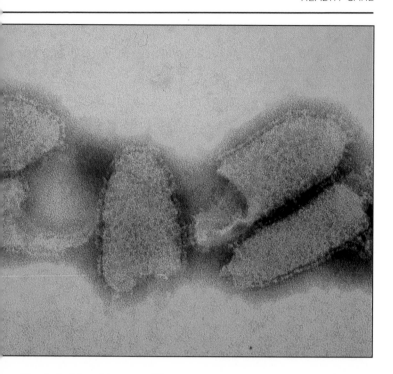

Regular bathing of the area will be required to remove the deposits, which otherwise can give rise to an infection.

Feline urinary disorders
Feline urolithasis: Also known as **feline urological syndrome (FUS),** this is a painful condition which is most often seen in male cats. It results from a blockage in the urethra which is the route by which urine leaves the body from the bladder. Difficulty in urination is a typical sign, and the cat will also show evident discomfort, licking repeatedly at the penile area.

It will be reluctant to squat to urinate and, depending on the extent of the blockage, may pass little or no urine. Since the bladder only has a finite capacity, rapid veterinary attention is required in order to remove the obstruction.

The actual cause of the condition is unclear. A viral involvement has been suspected, but any reduction in the cat's water intake can also be an underlying factor. As the urine then becomes more concentrated, so

Above: *An unusual view of the deadly rabies virus, seen under an electron microscope. It attacks the nervous system, and will prove fatal, both for animals and humans.*

there is a greater likelihood of the salts present in solution actually crystallizing out in the urinary tract, creating a blockage.

Your veterinarian may recommend dietary changes, notably a switch from dried foods, and the addition of a limited quantity of salt, to encourage fluid intake. It is also possible to make the urine more acidic, which lessens the possibility of urolithasis.

Female cats are less at risk from FUS, because their urethras tend to have a broader dimension. However, since this part of the urinary tract is shorter than in males, they are potentially more vulnerable to infections of the bladder, giving rise to the condition known as cystitis. This is also painful, but can be corrected by antibiotic therapy in most cases.

The presence of bladder stones is quite unusual in cats.

Older cats

The signs of ageing in cats are rather insidious, but there may be a loss of coat colour, and certainly their level of activity is likely to decline.

Dental problems may arise, and cause bad breath, although this will need to be distinguished from the effects of kidney failure, which has similar symptoms. This is inevitable over a period of time, as the functioning of the kidneys becomes impaired. Loss of appetite is another characteristic sign, and the extent of the renal (kidney) damage can be assessed reliably only by means of a blood test.

Manipulation of the diet may help to offset the worst of the damage, but a further progressive decline will be inevitable. The cat is likely to drink more, and weight loss may become increasingly apparent.

Apart from kidney failure, other possible causes exist for these symptoms in the elderly cat. They

Above: *Cats tend to become less active as they get older. If you notice that your cat develops bad breath, consult your veterinarian.*

Left: *Older cats tend to be less keen to wander far from home, even when the weather is good. They often live well into their teens.*

include a hyperactive thyroid, in which case the cat often eats more than normal, and diabetes mellitus. Neoplasia (cancer) is also more likely to be implicated in older cats, and your veterinarian will be able to advise you accordingly on the correct diagnosis.

It is always a very difficult decision to have your cat euthanased, but in the first place, you can discuss the situation frankly with your veterinarian. Clearly, there will be a point at which your cat is suffering, and at this stage, euthanasia will be the kindest option.

A case in point may be when a cat develops iliac thrombosis, with blood clots forming in arteries supplying the hind limbs. Sudden paralysis results, and although in some cases a brief respite will occur, further episodes are likely. Iliac thrombosis is often linked to failure of the heart muscle, known as cardiomyopathy, which enables the clots to form in the first instance.

Euthanasia is usually carried out by injection, and will be painless. The cat, given the drug which is related to the compounds often used for anaesthetic purposes, simply falls asleep, and its heart stops. If you wish, your veterinarian can arrange disposal of your pet's body, and there is no need to stay while the cat is euthanased. This may save you unnecessary anguish at this difficult and traumatic time.

EMERGENCY CARE

ESSENTIALS OF FIRST AID

The following pages are devoted to emergency situations which you may encounter as a cat-owner. Always remember that a cat which requires first aid is likely to be in pain, and needs to be treated carefully. It may well attempt to bite and scratch without hesitation, even though it is usually docile. This is particularly significant in areas where rabies is endemic. Veterinary help will almost inevitably be required in most cases, but rapid action by you in the first instance can make the difference between life and death. Even if you find that the cat is dead, notify the local animal rescue organisation, who may be able to trace the cat's owner. The police should also be informed. Always have a cat carrier to hand.

FIRST AID KIT

It is well worth having a small first aid kit available for use in emergencies. You may have to collect the items yourself, since first aid kits for cats are not available from most pet stores, although a few are now beginning to stock such things. The local pharmacy should be able to provide most if not all of your requirements.

- A small box of cotton wool is essential. Cotton wool buds are also useful, especially for cleaning your cat's ears, but take care not to cause injury by probing deep into the ear canal.

- Olive oil and liquid paraffin are versatile, being useful for cleaning the ears, as well as relieving cases of constipation and assisting the passage of furballs through the digestive tract. In order to dose your cat, you will require a 5ml teaspoon, such as the plastic ones dispensed with human medicines. This like other items in the first aid kit, should be kept exclusively for use with your cat.

- As an alternative, your veterinarian may supply you with a 5ml syringe, which, without a needle, makes an effective dispenser for such liquids. This enables the fluid to be run into the side of the mouth.

- A selection of crepe bandages should also be included in the first aid kit. Gauze and a roll of absorbent lint, which is applied directly to the wound with its fluffy side upwards, are also likely to prove useful. Other necessary items include a safe antiseptic for bathing the site of the injury, and safety pins and bandaging tape.

- A sharp pair of scissors is essential, and nail clippers can also be useful to cut away an overgrown or damaged claw. A styptic pencil is also useful, to stop any minor bleeding, as from a torn claw. Alternatively, you can use powdered alum dissolved in water, and applied directly to the wound on cotton wool, to control minor bleeding of this type.

- You should also have a small amount of sodium bicarbonate (baking soda) available, to relieve the irritation if your cat is stung. This again will need to be dissolved in water, so keep a small plastic container in the kit. A pair of flat-ended tweezers will be needed, to remove the sting left by a bee, or indeed a splinter or any kind.

- Poisoning requires rapid action, and it is worth having some washing soda included as an emetic in the emergency kit. This, like all other medicines, should be properly labelled. In order to remove paint and tar from the cat's paws or coat, you should keep a tin of waterless hand cleanser available.

- A clinical thermometer is always worth having to hand, to take your cat's temperature, along with a tube of lubricating jelly.

**A STEP BY STEP GUIDE TO FIRST AID
FOR ACCIDENTS AND EMERGENCIES**

MAJOR EMERGENCIES

MINOR EMERGENCIES

KITTEN EMERGENCIES

ROAD ACCIDENTS

1. Remove cat from immediate danger if at all possible.

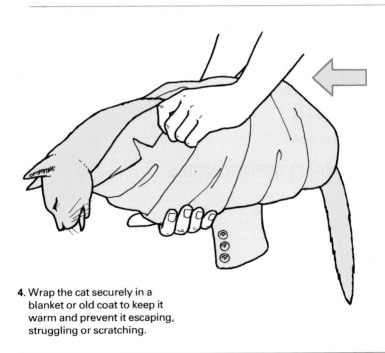

4. Wrap the cat securely in a blanket or old coat to keep it warm and prevent it escaping, struggling or scratching.

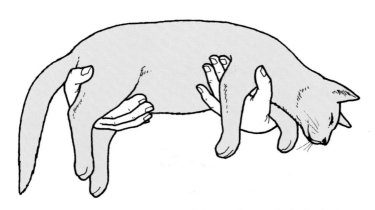

2. Do not tip or twist the body; keep flat to avoid putting pressure on internal injuries, such as a ruptured diaphragm.

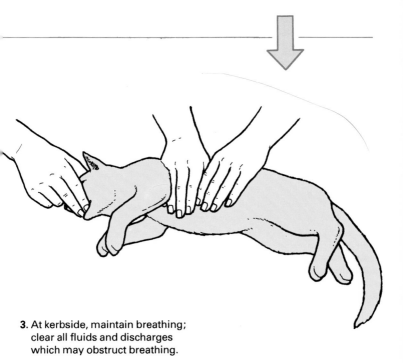

3. At kerbside, maintain breathing; clear all fluids and discharges which may obstruct breathing.

MAJOR EMERGENCIES

BLOOD LOSS

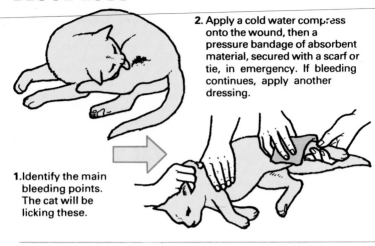

2. Apply a cold water compress onto the wound, then a pressure bandage of absorbent material, secured with a scarf or tie, in emergency. If bleeding continues, apply another dressing.

1. Identify the main bleeding points. The cat will be licking these.

BANDAGING A LIMB

1. To bandage a paw or tail lay the bandage down on one side of the paw and up the other, spiral down and back up, and tie off.

2. Bandage around injured limbs and secure above joint. Never use a pin: stick with tape.

3. Bandage the head either side of the ears, then cut a hole for each ear and pass over.

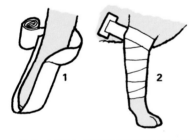

COLLAPSE AND SHOCK

1. Keep the cat dry, warm and comfortable. The head should be lower than the body to help blood to reach the brain.

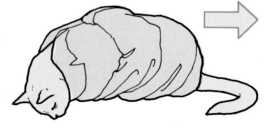

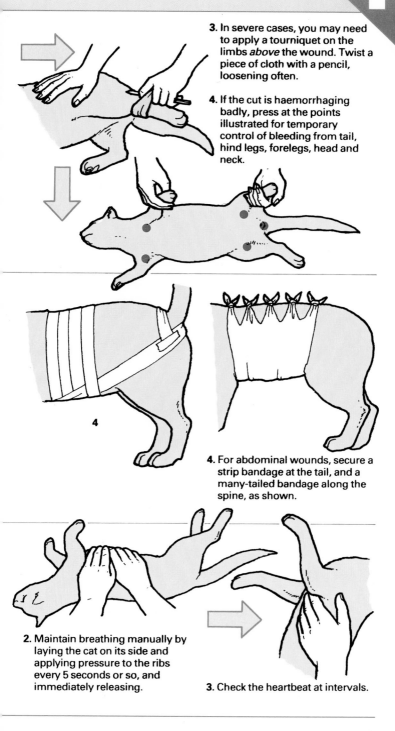

3. In severe cases, you may need to apply a tourniquet on the limbs *above* the wound. Twist a piece of cloth with a pencil, loosening often.

4. If the cut is haemorrhaging badly, press at the points illustrated for temporary control of bleeding from tail, hind legs, forelegs, head and neck.

4. For abdominal wounds, secure a strip bandage at the tail, and a many-tailed bandage along the spine, as shown.

2. Maintain breathing manually by laying the cat on its side and applying pressure to the ribs every 5 seconds or so, and immediately releasing.

3. Check the heartbeat at intervals.

FELINE UROLOGICAL SYNDROME (FUS)

FUS occurs in cats when the urethra is blocked by a gritty paste formed in the bladder. If ignored, FUS can be fatal.

1. An obvious sign of FUS is straining to urinate in a characteristic position with haunches slightly raised. The cat may cry out with the pain, and any urine passed may be blood-stained.

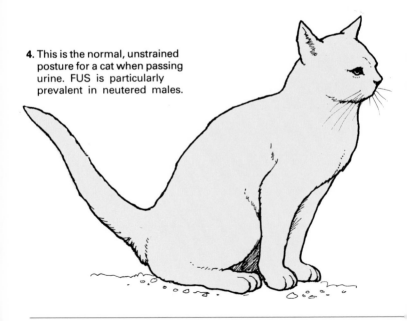

4. This is the normal, unstrained posture for a cat when passing urine. FUS is particularly prevalent in neutered males.

2. A cat with FUS will repeatedly lick the opening to the urethra. The vet may treat the condition with antibiotics or in severe cases a catheta may have to be inserted into the urethra. If untreated FUS can lead to kidney failure.

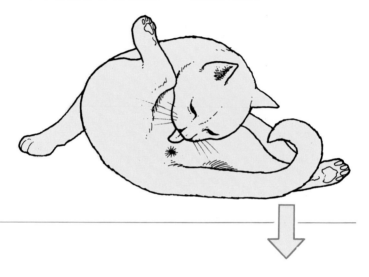

3. After treatment, provide the cat with plenty of moist foods and water to avoid recurrence.

MAJOR EMERGENCIES

DROWNING

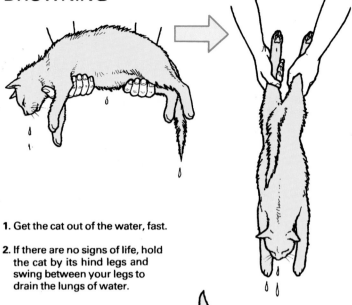

1. Get the cat out of the water, fast.

2. If there are no signs of life, hold the cat by its hind legs and swing between your legs to drain the lungs of water.

KNOWN POISONING

1. If the cat is seen to consume a noxious substance or human medicine, keep the container and show the vet what remains.

2. If the cat has *not* eaten anything corrosive, give a salt or soda solution. This acts as an emetic- it helps the cat to vomit. Phone the vet.

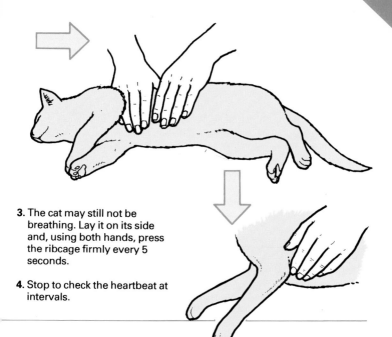

3. The cat may still not be breathing. Lay it on its side and, using both hands, press the ribcage firmly every 5 seconds.

4. Stop to check the heartbeat at intervals.

FOUR PREVENTABLE POISONING EMERGENCIES		
Poison	**Present in**	**Signs of poisoning**
Ethylene glycol	Anti-freeze	Loss of co-ordination, respiratory depression and kidney damage
Acetyl salicyclic acid	Aspirin	Vomiting, diarrhoea and convulsions
Warfarin	Rodent poisons, and rodents which may have eaten such poisons	Internal haemorrhaging and anaemia
Metaldehyde	Slug pellets and molluscs which have eaten them	Loss of co-ordination, profuse salivation, muscular twitches

In cases of corrosive poisoning you should not attempt to make your cat vomit. Telephone your vet for the correct treatment. Look on any packaging as appropriate for the chemicals concerned, rather than relying just on a brand name. This can save vital time.

MAJOR EMERGENCIES

CHOKING

1. Frequent choking when nothing is vomited is a serious sign.

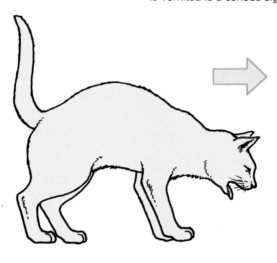

ELECTRIC SHOCK

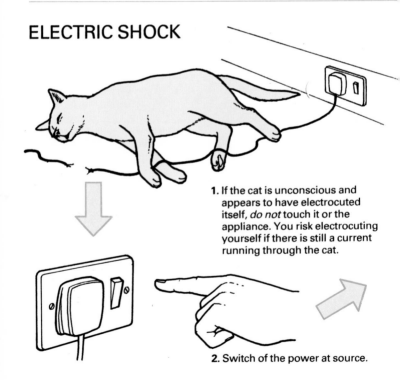

1. If the cat is unconscious and appears to have electrocuted itself, *do not* touch it or the appliance. You risk electrocuting yourself if there is still a current running through the cat.

2. Switch of the power at source.

2. The bone or other obstruction may be visible at the back of the throat. If the cat does not struggle too much, you may be able to remove the object with forceps (tweezers).

3. Alternatively, one person should hold the cat while the other removes the object.

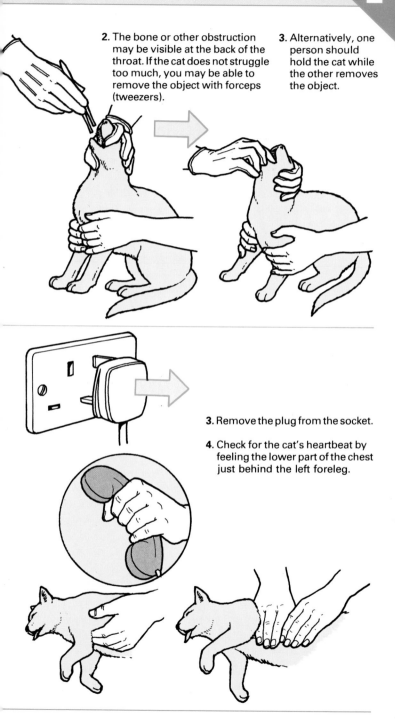

3. Remove the plug from the socket.

4. Check for the cat's heartbeat by feeling the lower part of the chest just behind the left foreleg.

BURNS AND SCALDS

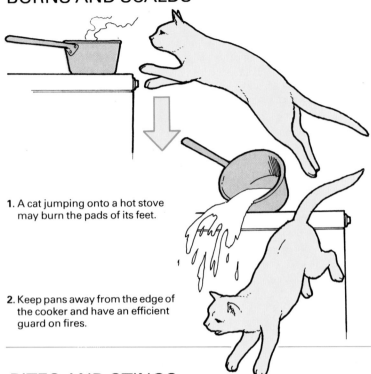

1. A cat jumping onto a hot stove may burn the pads of its feet.

2. Keep pans away from the edge of the cooker and have an efficient guard on fires.

BITES AND STINGS

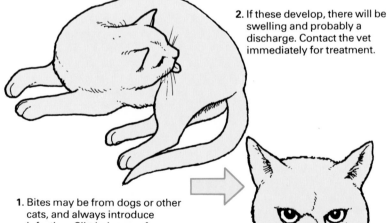

2. If these develop, there will be swelling and probably a discharge. Contact the vet immediately for treatment.

1. Bites may be from dogs or other cats, and always introduce infection. Clip hair away from area and bathe with hot water. Look carefully for hidden puncture marks which could become abscesses.

3. In the event of a burn or scald, *immediately* apply plenty of cold water to the burned skin. Then call the vet.

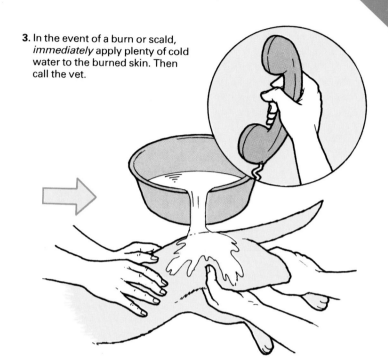

3. Bee stings are often visible protruding from the skin. Use a magnifying glass and forceps (tweezers) to remove the sting.

4. Stings mostly occur around the head and paws. They may produce swellings. If these are around the throat and restrict breathing, contact a vet.

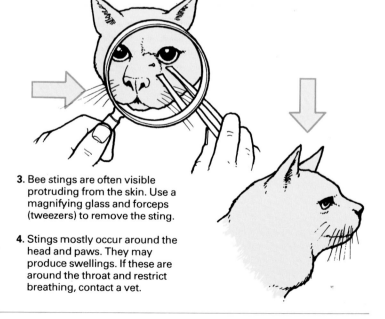

ABSCESSES

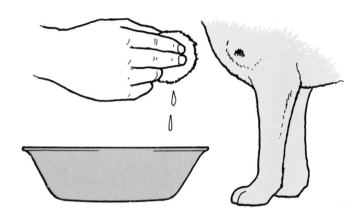

1. These swellings often result from a neglected cat bite. Bathing with cotton wool and warm water will bring the abscess to a head. Gently squeeze out any pus.

   If the abscess ruptures, bathe carefully with cotton wool. Antibiotics may be needed from the vet.

HYPOTHERMIA

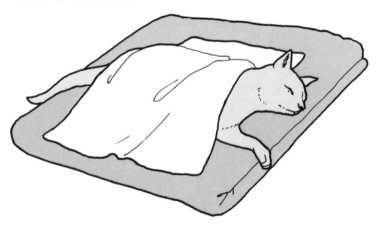

1. Cats are more resistant to extremes of temperature than dogs, but may still suffer from hypothermia, causing the body temperature to fall to a dangerously low level.

2. Remove the cat from the cold and insulate the animal with blankets to let its own body heat build up. *Do not give any alcohol!*

FOREIGN OBJECTS

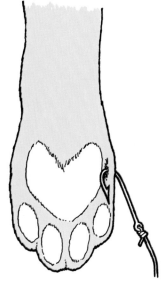

1. A fish hook imbedded in the mouth or paw can be removed by cutting the barb off first. While this is done the cat should be restrained, and may need sedation or even an anaesthetic.

2. A common problem in both the town and country is injury from airgun or shotgun pellets. These should be removed immediately by a vet.

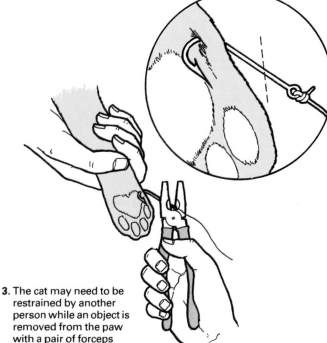

3. The cat may need to be restrained by another person while an object is removed from the paw with a pair of forceps (tweezers).

KITTEN EMERGENCIES

DELAY AT BIRTH

1. Do not neglect your queen as she goes into labour, but also do not fuss over her. This first stage may last many hours.

BIRTH POSITIONS

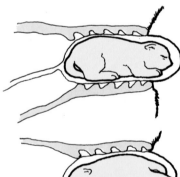

1. Most kittens will arrive head first. This is known as anterior presentation and is the easiest birth.

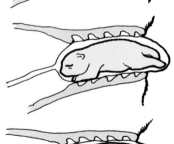

2. Posterior presentation, with the legs arriving first, does not usually present any major problems, unless the queen tires.

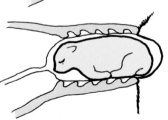

3. Problems are most likely to occur with breech births, when the hindquarters come first. The legs lie along the body, and may become trapped.

2. If she has been having strong contractions for more than two hours, you should call your vet for advice. Alert the vet anyway if it is the first litter.

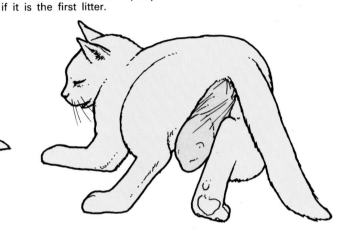

UMBILICAL HERNIA

1. A lump on a kitten's stomach, where the umbilical cord was attached, is the result of a weakness in the stomach wall, through which the intestine protrudes slightly. This may be hereditary, or result from an accident at birth.

NEARLY BORN AND STILL BORN KITTENS

1. If cutting the placenta, tie a ligature close to the body and very carefully cut the cord on the opposite side.

2. Dry the kitten briskly with a clean towel to stimulate breathing.

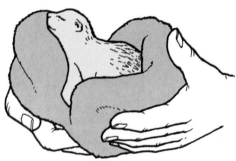

REARING ORPHANED KITTENS

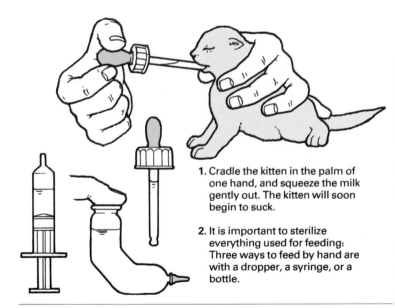

1. Cradle the kitten in the palm of one hand, and squeeze the milk gently out. The kitten will soon begin to suck.

2. It is important to sterilize everything used for feeding. Three ways to feed by hand are with a dropper, a syringe, or a bottle.

3. If it does not breathe within a few minutes, hold the kitten cradled in your hand and swing it sharply several times to clear the air passages.

4. Return the kitten to its mother as soon as it has revived a little, and encourage the mother to lick it. This will stimulate breathing.

KITTEN CHECK LIST	
4–6 Weeks	Begin to introduce solid food into the kittens diet. This can be canned food made soft and moist. Supplement gradually to the mother's milk. Feed to appetite.
6–8 Weeks	Now fully weaned, the kitten can be fed 4 meals a day, using ¼ – ½ of a 390g (13.7oz) can (approximately – according to appetite).
8–16 Weeks	Feed ¾ of a can per day divided into approximately 3 meals
4–5 Months	Feed about 1 can per day divided into 3 meals
6 Months	Feed according to appetite as before. Reduce the number of meals to 2

INDEX

FURTHER READING

Alderton, D., *The Cat,* Macdonald 1983.
Bush, B., *The Cat Care Question and Answer Book,* Orbis 1981.
Dunnill, M., *The Siamese Cat Owner's Encyclopaedia,* Pelham 1974.
Johnson, N.H. with Galin, S., *The Complete Kitten and Cat Book,* Robert Hale 1979.

Joshua, J.O., *Cat Owner's Encyclopedia of Veterinary Medicine,* TFH Publications 1979.
Loxton, H., *The Cat Repair Handbook,* Macdonald 1985.
Pond, G. and Raleigh, I. (editors), *A Standard Guide to Cat Breeds,* Macmillan 1979.

Richards, D.S., *A Handbook of
Pedigree Cat Breeding,* Batsford
1977.
Richards, D.S., *A Cat of Your Own,*
Salamander 1981.
Richards, D.S., *An Illustrated Guide to
Cats,* Salamander 1982.
Robinson, R., *Genetics for Cat
Breeders,* Pergamon Press 1977.

Tottenham, K., *Looking after Your Cat,*
Ward Lock 1981.
Viner, B., *The Cat Care Manual,*
Stanley Paul 1987.
Watson, M.D., *Encyclopedia of
American Cat Breeds,* TFH
Publications 1978.
Wright, M and Walters, S. (editors),
The Book of the Cat, Pan Books 1980.